"UNLESS THE LORD BUILDS THE HOUSE..."

(God's Plan For The Home)

by

ROD AND BRENDA RUTHERFORD

**"Unless the Lord builds the house,
They labor in vain who build it;
Unless the Lord guards the city,
The watchman stays awake in vain."
(Psalm 127:1)**

**6477 Hugh Willis Road
Powell, TN 37849
rodrutherford@comcast.net**

DEDICATION

**We dedicate this book on the Christian home
to our children and their marriage partners
who are all Christians and have
raised their children in the faith:
Our daughter, Debra and her husband, Mark Davis
Our son, Kevin, and his wife, Vicky
Our son, Brett, and his wife, Joanne**

INTRODUCTION

Writing a book on the home as God created it has long been on our minds. Family members and friends have encouraged us to write such a book. We feel the time has come when we must get it done while we still have the physical and mental ability to do so. It is our prayer that it will be the crowning act of our lives together in God's service.

The reader may rightly inquire, "Who are these writers? What knowledge, special training or professional expertise do they have which qualifies them to teach others about such an important subject as the home and family?" In reply, we freely admit we are not psychologists, sociologists nor academically trained professional marriage counselors. We claim no special training in these fields. However, we firmly believe we have something to offer on the subject of marriage and stable Christian homes for the following reasons: First, it was our privilege to grow up in stable homes where our parents believed in God and His Son Jesus Christ, held the Bible in reverence as the authoritative, inerrant Word of God, and taught us by word and example that God intended for marriage to be between a man and a woman and involved a life-long commitment. Second, we have been happily married to one another at this writing for fifty-seven years. We are the proud parents of three faithful Christian children who are married to faithful Christians and have raised their children in the church of the Lord. Two of our eight grandchildren are now married to faithful Christians and we have been blessed so far with a great-grandchild. Surely, this has given us some useful knowledge and practical experience to share with others.

However, we believe our greatest qualification for writing a book on the home and family is that we both have been diligent, life-long students of God's Book, the holy Bible, and dedicated teachers of it to others. We believe the claims of the sacred Scriptures to be the inspired, inerrant, authoritative Word of God by which every accountable human being will be judged at the Last Day. We unhesitatingly accept the Bible's claims that it is God's guide for how we are to live our lives in this world.

We believe the gracious God who lovingly formed man from the dust of the earth and woman from the side of man has all the knowledge and wisdom necessary to know the needs and desires of His creatures. Further, we believe our Creator desires our happiness and well-being. For this reason He has given us the Scriptures to guide us. The Scriptures are therefore the "operator's manual" for mankind. God made man and woman and ordained marriage for their happiness. In His Word, He has supplied all the instructions necessary to have successful marriages and happy homes. No amount of training in psychology, sociology or counseling can compensate for or replace the Divinely given teachings of the Bible, the Creator's instruction manual for man.

That the home as God ordained it is in trouble today will not be denied by anyone who is even remotely acquainted with the facts. A century ago divorce was relatively unknown. Marriage was universally held in honor as a sacred trust. Today, we have come to the place where divorce is so easily obtained, and so few really respect God's teaching on marriage, that an increasing number of couples simply live together without the legal covenant and spiritual commitment of marriage. The "nuclear family" (a man and a woman legally married to one another with their children) is in danger of extinction according to some and must be replaced by alternate forms of marriage such as polygamy, same sex marriage, communal marriage, serial marriages, marriage to children, and even to animals according to others. When God's plan is given up, there is no limit to the depths into which man will descend (Read Romans 1:18-32). Many other nations besides the United States are traveling the same road of disobedience which results in destruction by their blatant disregard for God's plan for the home.

It will be our aim in this book to set forth the plain teaching of God's Word on marriage and the family, to make specific applications to pressing needs and concerns, and to share from our lifetime of study and experience practical suggestions and advice to help make our homes what God intends for them to be - a foretaste of Heaven on earth!

ABOUT THE AUTHORS

Rod and Brenda Rutherford were privileged to grow up in the churches of Christ. They obeyed the Gospel in their early teenage years and have been active in the Lord's work since that time. They met while attending a Christian college where their common desire to be missionaries drew them together. They married while in college and are blessed to have shared fifty-seven years together. They have also been blessed with three children, eight grandchildren and one great grandchild (as of this writing).

Rod and Brenda consider their greatest blessing to be that all of their children and their marriage partners, and their married grandchildren and their marriage partners, are active Christians. Their daughter, Debra, has taught small children in Bible classes since the age of twelve. Their two sons are both full-time preachers of the Gospel. Kevin has preached for churches in Mississippi, Minnesota, Missouri and North Carolina for more than thirty years. Brett has preached for the past twenty-five years years in mission fields in Wisconsin and Tasmania (Australia). A grandson, Caleb, is a full-time preacher of the Gospel. Another grandson, Mitchell, plans to enter South East Institute of Biblical Studies to prepare for a lifetime of preaching in Australia.

The Rutherfords live in Powell, Tennessee where they are active members of the Karns church of Christ and spend their time writing.

SPECIAL THANKS

We are indebted to our son, Kevin, and his wife, Vicky, and to our son, Brett, and his wife, Joanne, for reading the book, making corrections and offering valuable suggestions for improvement. Producing a book entails months (sometimes years) of hard work. It takes more than just a writer or writers to produce a book. In many ways, the production of this book has been a team effort.

TABLE OF CONTENTS

The Title Page

Dedication

Introduction

About the Authors & Special Thanks

Table of Contents

Chapter 1:   IN THE BEGINNING

There are three institutions which are fundamental to all of society. Each of these institutions was ordained by God for the specific functions it serves. The civil government was ordained by God to insure peace, security and order in society. It is essential for civilization to exist. Otherwise, there would be anarchy and society would revert to the law of the jungle (Romans 13:1-7). God works through governments of men, regardless of whether they may be monarchies or democracies to bring about His will (Daniel 4:17; Acts 17:26-28). He does not condone the evil deeds of rulers but will hold them accountable for their actions (Genesis 18:22-32; Romans 2:5,6).

The church of Christ is an essential institution provided by Almighty God to fill the spiritual needs of man for salvation. It was prophesied in the Old Testament, prepared by John the immerser, and purchased by the blood of Jesus the Christ (Joel 2:28-32; Isaiah 2:1-3; Daniel 2:44; Mark 1:1-8; Acts 2:1-47; 20:28; 1 Corinthians 15:24-26).

The home, however, was the first of these three essential institutions ordained by God for the good of man. The home is the basic building block of all human society. Nations are composed of homes and are only as strong, good, decent, and well ordered as the homes which are in them. The church also is made up of homes. It is also only as strong, faithful and effective as the homes represented in it. If we want to solve the myriad of problems facing the nation, as well as those facing the church, we must begin with the home. As goes the home, so goes the nation and the same can be said of the church. The failure of homes to teach reverence for God, respect for authority and the principles of decency and righteous living is at the heart of the turmoil and strife in society, and the division, immorality, and lack of respect for God's Word in the church.

The home (family, marriage) is as old as the human race. It came into being on the sixth day of creation, the same day God created man (Genesis 1:27; 2:1-25). The home did not evolve as some social scientists tell us, but it was a direct creation of God. After He had made the man, Adam, from the dust of the ground, God placed him in the Garden of Eden to "tend and keep it." God saw that it was not good for the man to be alone. He said, 'I will make him a helper comparable to him'" (Genesis 2:18, NKJV). God then caused all the animals to pass before Adam and he named them. However, the statement is made: "But for Adam there was not found a helper comparable to him" (Genesis 2:20).

Perhaps we may wonder why an animal could not have been a suitable companion for man. There are several factors to consider. First, God ordained that every living thing, whether human, animal or plant should "bring forth after its kind" (Genesis 1:11,12, 21, 24, 25). Contrary to what the false hypothesis of evolution says, one "kind" does not evolve into a different kind. A fish never becomes a bird nor does a monkey become a man. Each kind created by God was commanded to multiply and fill the earth (Genesis 1:22-27). Humans are a different kind from animals so they cannot mate with them and produce offspring. In fact, God condemns sexual relations between a human being, whether male or female, and an animal. He calls it "perversion" (Leviticus 18"22-25).

Second, animals belong to a lower form of creation than man. Animals cannot speak, reason, laugh, appreciate the beauties of nature, music, art and literature, or read and reason. They cannot harness the environment around them for their good except for obeying basic instincts such as hunting for food or building a nest. Intellectually, morally, emotionally, spiritually and aesthetically, animals are not comparable to mankind.

Third, another reason that animals are not suitable to be "a helper comparable to man" is that man is made in the image of God (Genesis 1:27). What is this image of God that man bears? It is not man's physical nature for God is not a physical being as man is. Jesus said: "God is Spirit, and those who worship Him must worship Him in spirit and in truth" (John 4:24). Jesus further tells us that "a spirit does not have flesh and bones" (Luke 24:39). The image of God that man bears is the spirit which dwells in man's physical body. It is his from conception and leaves his body only at death. It returns to his physical body when it is raised from the dead at the Last Day. The spirit and body are reunited and transformed into a body suited to inherit eternity in the Heavenly Kingdom.

> "So God created man in His own image; in the image of God He created him; male and female He created them" (Genesis 1:27).

> "Then the dust will return to the earth as it was, and the spirit will return to God who gave it" (Ecclesiastes 12:7).

> "The burden of the Word of the Lord against Israel. Thus says the Lord who stretches out the heavens, lays the foundation of the earth, and forms the spirit of man within him" (Zechariah 12:1).

> "Now may the God of peace Himself sanctify you completely; and may your whole spirit, soul, and body be preserved blameless at the coming of our Lord Jesus Christ" (1 Thessalonians 5:23).

One should also read carefully Luke 16:19-31; 23:39-43; John 20:17; 1 Thessalonians 4:13-17; 1 Corinthians 15:20-26, 50-55; James 2:26).

When animals die they simply cease to exist. Their bodies return to the dust. They do not have a spirit; therefore there is no part of them which lives on. Man needed a "helper comparable to him," that is, he needed a companion who was made in the image of God as he was. That image is the spirit, the Godlike part of man which dwells in him and leaves his body at death, but is reunited with his body when the dead are raised at the Last Day. Only another human being who also bore the image of God was suited to be a "helper comparable" to man.

The special creation of woman to be a helper comparable to man occurred on the sixth day of creation. It was the crowning act of God's creation. God caused Adam to fall into a deep sleep. He then took a rib from the side of Adam and from it He fashioned the woman. As the old English commentator, Matthew Henry, observed: "That the woman was made of a rib out of the side of Adam; not made out of his head to rule over him, nor out of his feet to be trampled upon by him, but out of his side to be equal with him, under his arm to be protected, and near his heart to be beloved."

It is worthy of observation that God did not make another man to be Adam's companion for two men "cannot be fruitful and multiply and fill the earth." The Bible condemns the sin of homosexuality in no uncertain terms. The ancient cities of Sodom and Gomorrah were destroyed by God because of homosexuality (Genesis 19:1-26; Jude 7). The Law of Moses forbade homosexuality: "You shall not lie with a male as with a woman. It is an abomination" (Leviticus 18:22). The New Testament shows that the ultimate depths of sin when men refuse to have God in their knowledge results in homosexuality (Romans 1:18-28). However, one can repent of homosexuality just as he can repent of other forms of fornication, idolatry, cursing, stealing, coveting, lying, drunkenness, etc. Some who became members of the church at Corinth had been guilty of homosexuality and sodomy, but they were washed, sanctified and justified when they obeyed the Gospel (1 Corinthians 6:9-11).

When God brought the woman He had made to Adam, he said: "This is now bone of my bones and flesh of my flesh; she shall be called 'woman' because she was taken out of man" (Genesis 2:23). Following this statement of Adam, the Creator Himself proclaimed:

> "Therefore, a man shall leave his father and his mother and be joined to his wife, and they shall become one flesh" (Genesis 2:24).

In summary, we have learned the home is not an invention of man. It is not simply a matter of convenience or of culture. It did not evolve. It originated with the Creator of the universe. Marriage is for two people only, a man and a woman. In short, we may say that **God's original plan of marriage was one man, one wife, for life!**

In our next chapter we shall notice some deviations to God's original plan of marriage of one man, one wife for life. We will also see some "concessions" God made to His people during the Patriarchal and Mosaic ages because of their rebellion and the hardness of their hearts. These concessions were not part of His original intentions for marriage, nor were they designed to be permanent. We shall also see that Jesus restored God's original intention that marriage is for "one man, one wife, for life" but gave one and only one exception to it.

Review Questions

1. What are three institutions that are fundamental to all human society?

2. Who ordained these three institutions?

3. What is the purpose of civil government?

4. Why is the church of Christ essential?

5. Which one of these three essential institutions was created first?

6. What is the basic building block of all society?

7. Where must we begin if we are going to solve the problems confronting the nation as well as the church?

8. When did the home (marriage, family) come into being?

9. When God saw that it was not good for man to be alone, what did He say?

10. Why cannot animals be "helpers comparable to man?"

11. What are some things that man can do which are impossible for animals?

12. What was God's original law of marriage?

13. Where did Jesus get His marriage law?

14. What does man have that sets him apart from the animals?

15. How is man made in the image of God?

16. When does God put a spirit in man?

17. When does the spirit leave man's body? Where does it go?

18. Why were Sodom and Gomorrah destroyed by God?

19. What was the crowning act of God's creation?

20. Can one be forgiven of the sin of homosexuality? Give a Bible example.

21. How does God describe homosexuality in the Old Testament?

Chapter 2:   DEVIATIONS FROM THE ORIGINAL

Following the expulsion of Adam and Eve from the Garden of Eden because of their disobedience, sin soon became rampant in the world. Cain, the firstborn son of Adam and Eve, killed his brother, Abel (Genesis 4:8). Lamech, a descendant of Cain, confessed to his two wives, Adah and Zillah, that he had killed a man (Genesis 4:23,24). Lamech is the first recorded person in human history to deviate from God's original plan of marriage which was one husband and one wife for life (Genesis 4:19).

In time, polygamy (one man having many wives) became widely practiced. Even some men who were otherwise godly men of faith had multiple wives. Among these were such notable Bible characters as Abraham, Jacob, David and many others among the kings of Israel and Judah. However, it appears that monogamy (one husband and one wife), God's original plan for marriage, continued to be the norm. Many outstanding men of God such as Noah, Isaac, Aaron, Isaiah, Ezekiel, and Hosea were faithful to God's original plan as given in Genesis 2:24.

Under the Law of Moses another deviation from God's original plan was permitted (allowed but not preferred). According to Deuteronomy 24:1-4, if a husband found in his wife "some uncleanness", he was permitted to give her a writing of divorcement. She could then become another man's wife, but was forbidden to remarry her husband who had divorced her. The meaning of the "uncleanness" for which a divorce was permitted to be granted was widely debated in Jesus' day (Matthew 19:3). Some maintained that it referred to sexual impurity in some form. Others argued that it covered anything the wife did which displeased her husband even something as trivial as burning the bread.

Jesus did not address the meaning of "uncleanness" but said the reason God had permitted divorce was "because of the hardness of your hearts" adding "but from the beginning it was not so" (Matthew 19:8). J.W. McGarvey, outstanding Bible scholar of the past, suggested "...a positive prohibition of divorce would have led to promiscuous intercourse, or to secret assassination of wives who were displeasing to their husbands...." (J. W. McGarvey: Commentary on Matthew and Mark, pp. 164,165). In other words, McGarvey is suggesting that God permitted divorce as a protection for wives for if men were not allowed to divorce them they would either seek sexual fulfillment in others, or might mistreat their wives even to the point of killing them.

Some have suggested that God's condoning polygamy in the Patriarchal and Mosaic ages was like His allowing Israel to have a king when it was not His original intention they be governed that way. When Israel had conquered Canaan, God ruled them for three hundred years through judges who were chosen by Him. In time, the people became dissatisfied with God's government and wanted to be like the nations around them who were ruled by kings. When Samuel was growing old, and his sons that he had appointed as judges were not following his example of honesty and righteousness, the people came to him and demanded: "Now make us a king to judge us like all the nations."

Samuel was unhappy with the request of the people of Israel. He felt it was an affront to him and inquired of God what he should do. God told Samuel to heed the voice of the people and give them a king. He further said: "They have not rejected you but they have rejected me that I should not reign over them" (1 Samuel 8:1-9). Centuries later, God reminded Israel of their rebellion and stated: "I gave you a king in My anger and took him away in My wrath" (Hosea 13:11). When men's hearts are rebellious and they are determined to have their own way, God may sometimes allow us to have what we demand in order to teach us a lesson. We must remember that God's way is always best whether or not we like it or understand it.

We know that God still held to His original plan of marriage of "one man, one wife, for life" despite these temporary concessions because of the hardness of the hearts of some of His chosen people. In the book of Malachi, the last Old Testament book to be written, God's prophet reprimanded the Jews for leaving the wives of their youth and marrying heathen women. Malachi states in no uncertain terms: "For the Lord God of Israel says that He hates divorce" (Malachi 2:16)!

We can learn from the Old Testament what God is like and how He dealt with His people as He prepared to send His Son into the world (Romans 15:4; 1 Corinthians 10: 11; Galatians 3:24,25). However, the Old Testament as a binding law on God's people has been taken away. It ended when Christ died on the cross (Colossians 2:14; Ephesians 2:14-18; Hebrews 8:6-13). We now live under the new covenant of Jesus Christ (Hebrews 10:9).

In our next chapter we will learn what Jesus the Christ, God's Son, taught regarding marriage and divorce. We cannot have Christian homes unless they are built on the solid foundation of Christ's teaching (Matthew 7:24-27)!

REVIEW QUESTIONS

1. Who committed the first murder?

2. Which descendant of Cain was also a murderer?

3. Who was the first recorded polygamist?

4. Name some godly men in the Old Testament who were polygamists.

5. Name some godly men in the Old Testament who held to God's original plan for marriage.

6. Where in the Old Testament do we read of a concession permitting a man to divorce his wife if some "uncleanness" is found in her?

7. What were the thoughts of the Jews in Jesus' day regarding the meaning of "uncleanness" as a reason for a man putting his wife away?

8. Why did God allow this concession according to the Lord Jesus Christ?

9. What did J. W. McGarvey suggest as the reason that God permitted men under the Law of Moses to divorce their wives?

10. What Old Testament historical event suggests the possible reason God may have tolerated polygamy while still disapproving of it?

11. What were some of the men of Israel in the days of Malachi the prophet doing that aroused God's anger?

12. What was God's attitude toward divorce according to Malachi?

13. Whom did Israel reject as their ruler when they demanded they be given a king?

14. Why did Israel want a king?

15. When did the Old Testament as a binding law upon God's people end?

16. If a man divorced his wife under the Law of Moses, what one restriction was placed upon her?

17. Upon what must our homes be built if they are to be truly Christian?

18. Define polygamy. Define monogamy.

Chapter 3: BACK TO THE ORIGINAL

The Pharisees were a sect of the Jews who were very strict in small matters. However, they often overlooked more important matters. Jesus told them: "These you ought to have done, without leaving the others undone" (Matthew 23:23). The Lord also called the Pharisees "hypocrites" because they did not do what they taught others they must do (Matthew 23:1-14). The Pharisees were very jealous of Jesus. They envied His popularity with the people. Therefore, they constantly sought ways they could trap Him in His words or otherwise embarrass Him before the crowds who flocked to hear Him.

In Matthew, chapter 19, we learn of one occasion when the Pharisees sought to embarrass the Lord. They asked Jesus a question which was very controversial among the Jews: "Is it lawful for a man to divorce his wife for just any reason?" The Pharisees knew the Jews were divided on the question of the reason for divorce. Some of them believed Deuteronomy 24:1-4 gave a man permission to divorce his wife for almost any excuse. Others strongly disagreed. They said divorce was permitted only if a man's wife had committed adultery. The Pharisees knew Jesus would not please some of the people no matter what He answered because the people were divided.

The Lord answered the Pharisees' question by asking them a question: "Have you not read that He who made them at the beginning made them male and female, and said, 'For this reason a man shall leave his father and his mother and be joined to his wife, and the two shall become one flesh? So then, they are no longer two but one flesh. Therefore, what God has joined together, let not man separate'" (Matthew 19:4-6).

In this passage, the Lord taught four important facts about marriage as God ordained it. First, He said God made them male and female. Marriage is only for a man and a woman. God did not intend for a man to marry another man or for a woman to marry another woman. Homosexuality is a sin. It is a perversion of mankind as God made us. Those who practice homosexuality or sanction homosexual marriage will not go to Heaven unless they truly repent as the Corinthians did:

"Do you not know that the unrighteous will not inherit the kingdom of God? Do not be deceived. Neither fornicators, nor idolaters, nor adulterers, nor homosexuals, nor sodomites, nor thieves, nor covetous, nor drunkards, nor revilers, nor extortioners will inherit the kingdom of God. And such were some of you, but you were washed, but you were sanctified, but you were justified in the name of our Lord Jesus Christ and by the Spirit of our God" (1 Cor. 6:9-11).

Second, Jesus taught that "a man shall leave his father and his mother and be joined to his wife." When a man and a woman marry, it is God's plan that they leave the homes of their parents and establish their own home. The husband will then be the head of his own home. As the head, he will love his wife and provide for her and for the children who may be born to them (1 Timothy 5:8). His wife must respect, obey and submit to him as her head just as the church submits to Christ (Ephesians 5:22-33).

Third, Jesus taught that "the two shall become one flesh." God wants only two people in a marriage. Polygamy was not a part of God's original plan for marriage even though God tolerated it for a time in the Old Testament. The Lord Jesus Christ has restored God's original plan of "one man, one wife, for life."

Fourth, the Lord said: "What God has joined together, let not man separate." In a marriage acceptable to God, a man and a woman are joined together by God. When a man who is qualified Scripturally to marry and a woman who is qualified to marry according to God's law have complied with the laws of the state or nation in which they reside (Romans 13:1-7), they are thereby joined in marriage by God. In every marriage acceptable to God, three individuals are always involved: God, who made marriage and gave the laws to govern it, an eligible man, and an eligible woman. God is a witness to every such marriage covenant (Malachi 2:14-16). How dare anyone come between a couple married in God's sight! Anyone who breaks up a Scriptural marriage is defying Almighty God and will pay the penalty for his sin (Matthew 19:6; Hebrews 13:4)!

The Pharisees did not like Jesus' answer to their question. They had failed in the attempt to embarrass Him before the people. They did not like what He taught and began to argue with Him. They asked: "Why then did Moses command to give a certificate of divorcement and put her away?" The Lord answered: "Moses, because of the hardness of your hearts, permitted you to divorce your wives, but from the beginning it was not so!" (Matthew 19:7,8).

The Pharisees said Moses commanded divorce. Jesus corrected them. He pointed out that God did not command divorce but only permitted it. God permitted divorce under the Law of Moses only because of the hardness of their hearts. He permitted divorce to protect the wives from the cruelty of their hardhearted husbands who might do them serious injury if they were not allowed to divorce them. Jesus then added, "But from the beginning it was not so!" It was not God's original plan that a married couple be separated as long as they lived. God hates divorce (Malachi 2:16)!

Jesus then plainly stated His law of marriage and divorce: "And I say unto you, whoever divorces his wife except for sexual immorality (fornication) and marries another, commits adultery; and whoever marries her who is divorced commits adultery" (Matthew 19:9). Let us note several things that are plainly taught in this verse.

First, it is the Lord Jesus Christ, the only begotten Son of God, man's Savior and man's only hope of salvation who is speaking. He has all authority both in Heaven and on earth (Matthew 28:18). He will come again one day (Hebrews 9:28). He will raise the dead (John 5:28,29). He will then judge every accountable person who has ever lived. Not a single accountable person shall escape (John 5:22; Acts 17:30,31; 2 Corinthians 5:10). He will judge us by His Word (John 12:48). Our marriages will be judged along with everything else in our lives. "Marriage is honorable in all and the bed undefiled, but fornicators and adulterers God will judge" (Hebrews 13:4).

Second, Jesus taught if one divorces his wife for any other reason than sexual immorality (fornication), and marries another, he is committing adultery. He commits adultery because by God's law, he is still married to his wife. God joined him and his first wife together. No one has the right to separate them. Being still married in God's eyes, he has no right to marry another woman. The laws of our land reflect the will of the people, not God. Man's laws permit many things which the Word of God calls sin.

Third, Jesus teaches that if a man divorces his wife, or a woman divorces her husband (see Mark 10:11,12), the one who is divorced will commit adultery if he marries again since he is still married in God's sight to the original mate.

Fourth, Jesus teaches that there is one and only one exception to God's general law of marriage. If one's marriage partner commits sexual immorality (fornication), then the one who is innocent has the right to divorce the unfaithful partner and marry someone else. The right to divorce and remarry is given only to the innocent partner. It is not given to the guilty partner (Read Matthew 5:31,32). A partner who is guilty of fornication can be forgiven if he truly repents. If he repents, the innocent marriage partner may choose to reconcile with the guilty partner but he is not required by the Scriptures to do so. In that case, the guilty partner must remain unmarried in order to go to Heaven. The wise man wrote: "...the way of transgressors is hard" (Proverbs 13:15).

The New Testament was first written in the Greek language. In Greek, the word which is translated in the New King James Version as "sexual immorality" is "porneia." The older versions translate "porneia" as "fornication." This word includes adultery (sexual relations between a married person and someone to whom he or she is not married). It also includes what we commonly call fornication (sexual relations between two unmarried people). Porneia also includes homosexuality (two of the same sex involved in sexual relations) and bestiality (sexual relations with an animal). <u>A Greek-English Lexicon of the New Testament and Early Christian Literature</u> by William F. Arndt and F. Wilbur Gingrich defines porneia as including "every kind of unlawful sexual intercourse" (p. 699).

Jesus' disciples were surprised that His teaching on marriage and divorce was so strict. They said, "If such is the case of a man with his wife, it is better not to marry." They were not thinking properly. God intended for people to marry for life. Therefore, when one marries, he must be willing to remain with his marriage partner as long as both shall live. God's plan for marriage in the beginning was "one man, one wife, for life." Jesus restored God's original plan. This is God's plan for marriage for all people in all the world today. Only one exception was given to it (Matthew 19:9).

REVIEW QUESTIONS

1. Why did Jesus call the Pharisees hypocrites?

2. What question did the Pharisees ask Jesus in order to embarrass Him?

3. How did the Jews disagree about the meaning of "uncleanness" in Deut. 24:1-4?

4. How did Jesus answer the question of the Pharisees?

5. What was God's marriage law in the beginning?

6. When a man and a woman marry, should they remain a part of the home of either his or her parents or should they establish their own home?

7. How does God join a man and a woman in marriage?

8. What did the Pharisees ask Jesus in an attempt to get around His answer to their question?

9. Did God command the Israelites to divorce their wives if they found some "uncleanness" in them or did he simply "permit" them to do so?

10. Why did God permit the Israelites to divorce their wives?

11. What is Jesus' general law of marriage?

12. To whom does Jesus' law of marriage, divorce and remarriage apply?

13. Who will be our Judge at the Last Day?

14. What is the standard by which we will be judged?

15. Who will be judged on the Last Day?

16. What is the only exception Jesus gave to His law of marriage?

17. Is the right to divorce and marry again given to the guilty partner as well as the innocent partner?

18. If one marries a person guilty of adultery who has been divorced by his innocent partner, is he guilty of committing adultery? Why? or Why not?

19. What are the sexual sins included in the Greek word "porneia?"

Chapter 4: PRACTICAL APPLICATIONS OF GOD'S PLAN

The church of Christ in the ancient Greek city of Corinth was established by Paul on his second missionary journey (Acts 18:1-18). Paul later wrote two letters to this church which are included in the New Testament. The Christians at Corinth also wrote to Paul asking a number of questions pertaining to marriage, divorce and related matters. The answers Paul, by inspiration, gave to their questions are found in the seventh chapter of First Corinthians. The questions are not fully stated in the chapter but we can understand what they were by the answers Paul gave to them.

It is essential that we remember two facts regarding the church at Corinth. First, we must remember that Corinth was a wicked, idolatrous city. Many of the members of the Corinthian congregation were worshippers of idols before they became Christians (1 Corinthians 6:9-11). Second, we must remember that Christians were often persecuted for their faith by both Jews and pagans. Paul spoke of "the present distress" in 1 Corinthians 7:26. It is generally acknowledged by Bible scholars and commentators that this refers to a time of persecution which threatened the church. The lives of the Christians may have been in actual danger. Paul's answers to their questions apply to this time of stress and uncertainty. We may not be facing a time of persecution but the principles behind the answers Paul gave are relevant to us today also.

The questions the Christians in Corinth asked Paul appear to be: (1) Is it right to be married? (2) Are sexual relations between a husband and wife right or is it better that they abstain? (3) Should widows marry again? (4) Would it be better if married people separate? (5) Should a Christian who is married to a non-Christian (a pagan) continue in the marriage? (6) Should virgins marry or remain unmarried? (7) Should fathers permit their unmarried daughters to marry? (8) If Christian widows remarry, does it matter whom they marry, whether Christians or pagans? Some of these questions are very similar or overlap so we will answer them together as one.

The first question Paul deals with is, "Is it right to be married?" Some religions such as the Roman Catholic Church teach that celibacy is a holier state than marriage. Therefore, it is better to remain unmarried. The Bible does not teach this. God created marriage because "He saw that it was not good for man to be alone" (Genesis 2:18). Marriage is essential also for the propagation of the human race (Genesis 1:27).

In the first verse of this chapter Paul wrote: "It is good for a man not to touch a woman." However, this was written in view of "the present distress," the time of persecution facing the church. It would be easier during this time if Christians did not have the care and concern for a marriage partner. However, lest someone should misunderstand, Paul quickly added: "Nevertheless, because of sexual immorality, let each man have his own wife, and each woman have her own husband" (verse 2). The apostle then explained that husbands and wives should have sexual relations so they would not be tempted to commit fornication. Sexual relations are right and good between two people who are married to one another (Hebrews 13:4).

Paul next answered the questions: "Should widows marry again?" and "Should those who are unmarried marry?" We must not forget that Paul's answers to the Corinthians' questions were given in the light of a present or soon to come persecution. Paul replied: "But I say to the unmarried and the widows: it is good for them if they remain even as I am; but if they cannot exercise self-control, let them marry for it is better to marry than to burn with passion" (verses 8 and 9). It is easier in a time of persecution if one does not have a wife or children to worry about. But certainly it is not wrong for a widow to remarry nor is it wrong for a person who has never been married to get married. If an unmarried person has difficulty controlling his sexual desires, it is better for him to marry. Sexual desires must only be fulfilled in marriage between a husband and his wife. It is much better to be married than to be tempted to commit fornication.

Another question the Christians at Corinth had asked Paul was: "Would it be better if married couples separated?" The answer to this question is an unequivocal "No!" Paul wrote: "Now to the married I command, yet not I but the Lord: a wife is not to depart from her husband. But even if she does depart, let her remain unmarried or be reconciled to her husband. And a husband is not to divorce his wife" (verses 10 and 11). Marriage is for life! Those who are already married must remain together to be pleasing to God. A wife needs to stay with her husband. If she leaves him, she must remain unmarried. She has no right to marry another and it would be a sin for her to do so. Let it be understood that Paul is not giving another exception to Jesus' law of marriage and divorce found in Matthew 19:9. If a wife has already left her husband, she needs to be reconciled to him. Her husband has no right to divorce her.

Paul now answers the question: "Should a Christian who is married to an idolater remain with him?" Paul makes it very clear that if an unbelieving partner is happy to remain with the believer, then they should stay together (verses 12-16). However, if the unbeliever decides to depart (perhaps to save his life in the persecution), the believer must allow him to depart. He is "not under bondage" in such cases. This means that the believer is not so tied to his marriage partner that he must give up his faith in Christ to keep his marriage together. Paul is not giving another exception to Jesus' law of marriage and divorce given in Matthew 19:9 as some erroneously teach. Paul instead says it is good for the believer to remain with the unbeliever for two reasons: (1) He may convert his unbelieving partner to Christ; (2) The children born to this mixed marriage will have the opportunity to be brought up in the faith (verses 14-16).

The church at Corinth had asked Paul about virgins who were old enough to be married. Should they plan to marry or not? Should fathers give their consent for their daughters to marry? Under normal circumstances, the answer would be a definite "yes" to both questions. However, this was not a normal situation but a crucial and perhaps dangerous time as persecution loomed before them. Jesus had not directly dealt with these questions during His ministry on earth. Therefore, Paul, as an inspired apostle, gave his inspired judgment (verses 25-38).

Paul pointed out that because of the present distress, virgins would be better if they did not marry. One who is married has care and concern for his marriage partner. One who is unmarried has more time to serve the Lord. But it is not wrong for a virgin to marry. In those days, marriages were arranged by the parents. If a man had a virgin daughter who was reaching the point when she soon would be too old to be desirable for marriage, he should allow her to marry. If, on the other hand, the daughter is content to remain unmarried in her father's house, because of the present distress it was better for her to do so. Paul concluded by saying: "So then he who gives her in marriage does well, but he who does not give her in marriage does better" (verse 38).

Next, Paul addresses the specific question of Christian widows remarrying during this time of uncertainty and persecution. Is it best they marry at this time? First, Paul makes it clear that widows are eligible to remarry: "A wife is bound by law as long as her husband lives; but if her husband dies, she is at liberty to be married to whom she wishes, only in the Lord" (verse 39).

Why is a Christian widow commanded to "marry only in the Lord?" Why is this not also required of a Christian widower? We must not forget that Paul is answering specific questions about marriage that were asked during a time of distress. In those days, women had few rights. Husbands had almost complete control over their wives and children. If a Christian woman was married to an idol worshipper, it could be very difficult, even dangerous, for her in a time of persecution. She might be mistreated by her unbelieving husband. He might attempt to force her to give up her faith in Christ Jesus in order to save her life. This is very likely the reason that widows, but not widowers, were given this command. It was to protect those who would be at the mercy of a pagan husband.

It is always best for Christians to marry Christians, whether in times of peace or persecution. Christian parents should teach their sons and daughters that it is very important to marry in the true faith (Ephesians 4:4-6). Otherwise there is always the danger that the unbeliever will draw away the believer from the truth.

Should we find ourselves in the same situation today the Corinthian Christians were in when they wrote to Paul, the answers Paul gave to their questions would apply to us too. In our next chapter we are going to look at the supreme importance and absolute necessity of a Christian home being governed by love.

REVIEW QUESTIONS

1. Who established the church of Christ in Corinth?

2. Why did Paul write to the church in Corinth?

3. What kind of city was Corinth? Was it known for its faith and morality?

4. How can we know what the questions were that the church at Corinth had written to Paul?

5. Before they became Christians, what did many of the Corinthians worship?

6. What was happening or about to happen to the church at Corinth when Paul wrote to them?

7. Which verse in 1 Corinthians 7 is relevant to a correct understanding of the entire chapter?

8. Is it holier and more pleasing to God if a Christian remains unmarried?

9. Why would it be better to be unmarried during a time of persecution?

10. Why should each man have his own wife and each woman her own husband?

11. If one has difficulty controlling his sexual desires, what should he do?

12. Is it ever right to have sexual relations outside of marriage?

13. Did Paul give an additional reason for divorce and remarriage to that given by the Lord in Matthew 19:9?

14. Why should Christian parents encourage their children to marry only Christians?

15. In the light of "the present distress," why should widows marry only in the Lord?

16. In the light of "the present distress," why would it be best for virgins to remain unmarried?

17. If a Christian's marriage partner leaves him/her, is he free to remarry?

18. Give two reasons a believer married to an unbeliever must remain with his marriage partner.

Chapter 5: LOVE IS ESSENTIAL

A home without love is like a house without a roof, a well without water, or a tree in the summer without leaves. Love is essential for a family to be truly happy and well pleasing to God. God wants husbands to love their wives just as Christ loved His church and died for it (Ephesians 5:25-3; Acts 20:28). He wants wives to love their husbands and children (Titus 2:3-5). God wants children to love, respect and obey their parents (Ephesians 6:1-3). There is no happier place on earth than a home filled with love. There is no sadder place on earth than a home where love does not dwell.

Many people do not know what real love is. In English, we use the word "love" very loosely. We may say "God loves you" or a man may tell his wife "I love you." At the same time we may say "I love sweets," or "I love my new car." The New Testament was first written in Koine Greek which was widely spoken in the ancient world. Greek is a more exact language than English. It has several different words for love. Two of them, "phileo" and "agape", are found frequently in the New Testament. "Phileo" is the kind of love one has for his family and friends. "Agape" describes the love that God has for all men. It is a love of the will. It describes the feeling of good will one has for others even if they do not love him in return. If one has "agape" as God does, he will love all men. He may not like some but he will love them in the sense that he desires only the best for them.

The great chapter on love in the New Testament is First Corinthians thirteen. Someone observed of this beautiful chapter that it has been admired by everyone though the ages, but practiced by few. Paul uses the word "agape" here to describe the kind of love God desires us to have for one another. Some older versions of the Bible translate "agape" as "charity." This, however, does injustice to the meaning in our current English usage. We think of charity as the act of giving to the needy. It is true that charity grows out of love, but charity is not love (agape) as the apostle Paul uses it in First Corinthians thirteen.

The church at Corinth was made up of people from many different backgrounds. There were Jews who had always worshipped the true God. There were those from pagan backgrounds who had grown up worshipping idols. Likely there were people of means and social standing as well as the poor, and perhaps there were even slaves among the members. It is not surprising that conflicts would come. They were also divided because they followed their favorite preachers rather Christ (1 Cor. 1:10-17).

The church at Corinth was blessed by being richly endowed with miraculous gifts of the Holy Spirit (1 Corinthians 1:4-7). These miraculous gifts were given by the laying on of the apostles' hands (Acts 8:14-21; 19:6,7; Romans 1:11; 2 Timothy 1:6). Before the New Testament had been fully revealed and written, miraculous gifts served not only to confirm the message and the messengers, but also revealed God's will. This wonderful blessing, sadly, had become a source of jealousy and contention among the Corinthian Christians. The more spectacular gifts, such as that of speaking in tongues (languages they had not learned that were miraculously imparted to them), healing, and the working of various miracles were prized above others which may not have been as outward and showy.

In chapters twelve through fourteen, Paul discusses this cause of contention and shows that all these gifts came from the same Holy Spirit. They were not given only for the benefit of the person gifted with them but for the edification of all. That which should have been a source of unity among the Christians had been perverted and made a cause of division. After discussing the place and purpose of these gifts from the Spirit in chapter twelve, Paul closes this portion of the discussion by writing: "Desire earnestly the best gifts. And yet I show you a more excellent way." Chapter thirteen opens with a discussion of love, "the more excellent way."

In the first three verses of chapter thirteen, Paul speaks of the demands of this love. First, he said that if one could speak in the many languages of men and even that of angels, but lacked love, it was nothing. He compared it to a clanging cymbal. A cymbal is a musical instrument which must be used in harmony with other instruments to produce a pleasing sound. When played alone, a cymbal is just an unpleasant and irritating noise. The special gift of languages was wonderful if one had love for his fellow Christians and used it for edifying them, but if not, it was just a worthless sound.

Second, Paul mentions another three of the special gifts given by God's Spirit. Prophecy was the miraculously imparted teaching of God's Word. It included the ability at times to foretell future events. Mysteries described portions of God's Word that had not yet been revealed. The faith to move mountains was miraculous faith (1 Corinthians 12:9; Matthew 17:20; 21:21). This miraculous faith was different from the faith which everyone must have in order to become a Christian. This kind of faith is not miraculous and comes from hearing God's Word (Romans 10:17). If one possessed all of these amazing gifts, it would be worthless if he did not have love.

Third, Paul said that if one gave up all he owned in order to help those in need, it would not please God unless he did it because of love. It is good to feed the hungry, provide clothing and shelter to the homeless, care for widows and orphans etc. In fact, we cannot practice pure religion and be pleasing to God if we fail to do these things (Matthew 25:31-46; James 1:27; Galatians 6:10). However, if we do not help others out of love, then God will not bless us for our good deeds.

Next, Paul defines love by describing it. He tells us that "love suffers long." If we love others, we will be patient with them. We will be kind to them even if they are unkind to us. We will imitate Jesus "who, when He was reviled, did not revile in return" (1 Peter 2:23).

Paul says that "love is kind." This means that if we truly love others, in our dealings with them we will be gentle and compassionate. "Be kind to one another, tenderhearted, forgiving one another even as God in Christ forgave you" (Ephesians 4:32).

Love "does not envy." One who is envious or jealous of others when good things happen to them does not love them. The leaders of the Jews killed Jesus because they were envious of Him (Matthew 27:18). Cain killed his brother, Abel, because he was envious of him (1 John 3:11,12). If we love others, we will not envy them but will rejoice at their success.

"Love does not parade itself." This means that if one really loves others, he will not boast about himself and what he has done. He will not think he is more important than others, He will be humble because he knows that "God resists the proud, but gives grace to the humble" (1 Peter 5:5).

If one truly loves others, he will not think he is better than they are. Paul said: "Love is not puffed up." It is not proud. Jesus told of two men who went into the temple to pray (Luke 18:9-14). One was a Pharisee who was very proud. Pharisees were held in high esteem among the Jews. The Pharisee, Jesus said, "stood thus and prayed with himself." He actually boasted to God about his good deeds and then had the audacity to thank God that he was not like the tax collector standing nearby. Tax collectors were universally hated among the Jews for they worked for the Romans who had subjugated the Jews and collected taxes from them. Tax collectors often were dishonest and collected more than what was just in order to fill their own pockets. This tax collector, however, was different. He feared God and felt himself unworthy even to approach God. In his sorrow for his sins, he smote himself on his chest and prayed, "God, be merciful to me, a sinner." Jesus said: "This man (the tax collector) went down to his house justified rather than the other."

"Love does not behave itself rudely." If one truly loves others, he will be polite and courteous to them. (1 Peter 3:8). Good manners are the natural result of love toward others. Love will practice "the Golden Rule" (Matthew 7:12).

"Love does not seek its own." Love is unselfish. One who loves others will put their welfare ahead of his. Paul wrote to the church at Philippi: "Let each of you look out not only for his own interests, but also for the interests of others" (Philippians 2:4).

"Love is not provoked." Love is not quick tempered. It does not have a short fuse. One will not become angry or irritated easily at the weaknesses and mistakes of others. A grouchy, irritable, easily upset person shows a lack of love.

"Love thinks no evil." This is translated from a Greek term which means "to write in a ledger." It is an accountant's term. If one loves another he will not keep a record of the bad treatment he has received from him. Sometimes married couples fuss and fight. They each may bring up the transgressions of the other from the past that were supposed to have been forgiven and should have been forgotten. This demonstrates a lack of real love.

"Love does not rejoice in iniquity." If one has love, he will not take pleasure in bad things. He will not want to hear the worst about other people nor will he rejoice when bad things happen to those he does not like.

"Love rejoices in the truth." If one loves others, he will be glad to know they are following in the way of truth. John wrote to the elect lady: "I rejoiced greatly that I have found some of your children walking in truth, as we received commandment from the Father" (2 John 4).

"Love bears all things." One will love others even when the love is not returned. He will even suffer insults and wrongs without retaliation for "love will cover a multitude of sins" (1 Peter 4:8).

"Love believes all things." If one has love, he will trust completely those he loves. He will be slow to criticize them and will not accept accusations about them unless he absolutely knows they are true.

"Love hopes all things." A little boy in school in England many years ago was a slow learner. A visitor came to the school one day. The teacher made a point of telling the visitor that Adam Clarke was "the stupidest boy in school." The visitor was a kind man. He said to the little boy whose feelings were wounded: "Never mind. You may become a great scholar some day. Do not become discouraged." Adam Clarke did indeed become a great scholar. He studied forty different languages and was conversant especially with the languages of the Bible. He is still well known today, two hundred years later, for a commentary he wrote on the entire Bible. It has remained in print since he wrote it and is still widely used.

"Love endures all things." If one has love he will suffer ill treatment without anger or hatred. He will persevere with family and friends and be patient with them when they are difficult and disagreeable.

"Love never fails." Love is an eternal virtue beginning with God. It will never end but will endure in Heaven throughout the ceaseless ages.

Paul next speaks of the duration of love and contrasts the possession of the gifts of the Spirit which the Corinthians valued so highly with love. The miraculous gifts were only temporary. They are like the scaffolding when a great building is erected. They are necessary while construction is going on but once it is completed, the scaffolding is removed for it is no longer needed. These gifts were temporary, but were removed once the New Testament had been completely revealed for they were no longer needed. Tongues, healing, prophecy and the other gifts ceased when the perfect (complete) had come. No longer was the church dependent upon partial revelation but the time came when "all things that pertain to life and godliness" had been given (2 Peter 1:3). The church possessed "the faith once for all delivered to the saints" (Jude 3). They had "the perfect law of liberty" (James 1:25). The close of the last book of the New Testament warned of those who would add to or take from that holy Book, the New Covenant of our Lord, which will guide us until He comes again (Revelation 22:18-21).

Although miraculous gifts have passed away, faith, hope and love continue. Faith is essential to being a Christian. We cannot please God unless we believe "that He is and that He is a rewarder of those who diligently seek Him" (Hebrews 11:6). Jesus said: "… if you do not believe that I am He, you will die in your sins" (John 8:24). When we get to Heaven, faith will be fulfilled in sight and will no longer be needed.

Hope is a great blessing which we as Christians have. It is "the anchor of the soul" (Hebrews 6:19). We hope for eternal life (Titus 1:2) and have it now in prospect and promise (1 John 2:25; 3:2,3). Hope is not yet realized in its fulness, but it will be when we get to Heaven (Romans 8:24).

In contrast to faith and hope, love will never end. It is essential that Christians love one another and their fellow men on earth and love God and His Son now and in eternity. There will never be a time when the saved will not love.

We have learned from the great apostle Paul in First Corinthians thirteen that love is even more important than the temporary possession of miraculous gifts from the Holy Spirit given by the laying on of the hands of the apostles of Christ. We have also learned that love will continue when faith is fulfilled in sight and hope is realized in actual possession of that for which we have hoped. We have also learned what love really is, what it is like, and what it will do if we possess it.

Applied to our homes and family, love will cause us to be kind, considerate, courteous, compassionate, unselfish, patient, cheerful, hopeful and treat others as we ourselves want be treated. It will be our fondest desire to do what is best for other family members. The result will be that our homes will become an outpost of Heaven in which we will enjoy a temporary foretaste of that which all the saints will enjoy in Heaven forever. Such love will cause the world to marvel. Others will see Christ in our homes.

REVIEW QUESTIONS

1. What is essential if a family is to be happy and please God?

2. What should be the happiest place on earth?

3. What often is the saddest place on earth?

4. What are two Greek words used in the New Testament for love?

5. What is the meaning of "phileo"?

6. What is the meaning of "agape"?

7. Which kind of love does God have for us?

8. Which kind of love is spoken of in 1 Corinthians 13?

9. What are the three abiding virtues mentioned in 1 Corinthians 13?

10. Will faith continue forever? If not, when will it be fulfilled?

11. Will hope continue forever? If not, when will it be fully realized?

12. Which one of the these three cardinal virtues will endure throughout the ages?

13. How were miraculous gifts of the Holy Spirit given?

14. How long were they to last?

15. What was the purpose of miraculous gifts?

16. Do miraculous gifts of the Holy Spirit continue today?

17. What is "that which is perfect"?

18. How did a visitor at Adam Clarke's school demonstrate real love to the boy?

19. A home without love may be compared to which three things?

20. Do homes where there is fussing, fighting, selfishness and rudeness demonstrate the love of Christ?

Chapter 6: COUNTING THE COST

Jesus taught the importance of counting the cost before becoming His disciple. Temptations, trials, disappointments and discouragements must be endured if one is to follow Him.

"If anyone comes to Me and does not hate (love less) his father and mother, wife and children, brothers and sisters, yes, and his own life also, he cannot be My disciple, and whoever does not bear his cross and come after Me cannot be My disciple" (Luke 14:26,27).

Jesus taught two parables to emphasize His point. First, He said no man who is wise will undertake a major building project without long range planning including having sufficient funds on hand to see the project through. Otherwise, he might have the building half completed when he ran out of money and had to abandon it. From that time forward, the half completed structure would stand as a testimony to his poorly planned undertaking, and he would be ridiculed for his failure.

Second, Jesus taught a parable about a king going to war against another king. If he has any common sense and understanding of military strategy, he will realize that if he goes against an army that is twice the size of his, he is inviting disaster and certain defeat. Therefore, he will negotiate a peaceful settlement rather than having himself and all his men killed by the poorly planned enterprise (Luke 14:31-32).

Whatever tasks in life one may undertake require planning and preparation to insure their success. This is most assuredly the case if one is planning to marry and establish a truly Christian home. In the past, as well as in some cultures today, marriages are commonly arranged by the parents. Choosing a lifetime marriage partner is considered to be much too important to be left to the young and inexperienced in life.

Today, in most modern cultures, young men and women have complete freedom to choose their lifetime partners. Sadly, all too many young people have had no specific training on how to choose the right partner, nor little idea of the responsibilities of marriage and raising a family. More and more people are growing up in single parent homes and have not had the opportunity of experiencing a fully functioning family with the interaction of a father and mother with one another and with their children. Others may have had the privilege of growing up in a fully intact family, but their parents have not set a proper example before them, nor have they made any effort to teach them about marriage and the family as God planned it.

This lack of example and void of preparation for marriage is at the heart of the worldwide divorce epidemic. It is essential that preparation be made for the lifetime commitment of marriage for it is second in importance only to our commitment to became a disciple of Christ and remain faithful to Him.

We shall note several essential areas of preparation which must be made to insure that we have a marriage which pleases God, guarantees our happiness, and is an example to those around us.

First, one must prepare himself for marriage. In order to choose the right person, one must be the right kind of person! Those who have had faithful Christian parents and godly grandparents should have a big head-start to being the right kind of person. In order to be the right kind of person, one must first of all be right with God. In short, he must be an active, faithful Christian who "seeks first the kingdom of God and His righteousness" (Matthew 6:33). One should be striving to live a life that is holy in thought, in word and in deed. Peter admonishes Christians to be holy "as He who called you is holy, you also be holy in all your conduct, because it is written: 'Be holy for I am holy'" (1 Peter 1:15,16).

Second, one who is holy will keep his body clean from the contamination of alcohol, nicotine, and other harmful addictive drugs such as marijuana, cocaine, etc. One will also strive to keep his mind clean from evil, impure thoughts and deeds. Pornography, whether in print or on a movie, computer or television screen, must be strictly and strenuously avoided. The wise man wrote: "Keep your heart with all diligence, for out of it spring the issues of life" (Proverbs 4:23).

Third, one who prepares properly for marriage will keep himself sexually pure. Sexual relations were created by God for companionship, satisfaction of sexual desire, expression of love, pleasure, and for procreation. However, God ordained that sexual relations are only to be engaged in between a man and a woman who are committed to one another for life in the bonds of marriage. Sexual relations between any others are sinful (Galatians 5:19-21). "Marriage is honorable among all, and the bed undefiled: but fornicators and adulterers God will judge" (Hebrews 13:4)!

Fourth, to be truly prepared for marriage one must remember the Bible teaching that God's simple plan for marriage is "one man, one wife, for life" (Genesis 2:18-24). Jesus restored God's original plan and gave one (and only one) exception to the general rule (Matthew 19:3-12). Note particularly verse 9 which states the one exception which permits divorce with the innocent party having the right to remarry without sin.

A veteran preacher of the Gospel stated that in his many years of experience, not one person in ten who asked him to officiate at their wedding knew and understood Jesus' teaching regarding marriage, divorce and remarriage. One must never forget that marriage is a lifetime commitment. It must not be entered into lightly or ended for just any reason.

The elders of the church must see that boys and girls in their early teenage years are taught God's plan and purpose for marriage. Preachers must frequently preach from the pulpit the requirements and obligations of marriage in God's sight. Visitors and newly baptized Christians need to be grounded in these essentials. Members of all ages must also be reminded frequently of God's will in regard to marriage (2 Peter 1:12-15). Parents in the home especially need to stress what the Bible says about marriage, divorce and remarriage and indoctrinate their children in the meaning of marriage and its responsibilities.

Fifth, one must choose his companions, especially his closest friends, very carefully. We live in the world, but we must not be of the world (1 John 2:15-17). The person one will eventually marry will most likely be someone he has met at school or work or during social or recreational activities. A faithful Christian man, who is married to a dedicated and active Christian wife, confessed to the elders of the congregation he and his wife attended that he was in his fourth marriage. He went on to explain that he was brought up in a worldly home. He married his first three wives when he was in the world. He met them in worldly places such as bars and clubs. He was faithful to each wife, but each of his first three wives was unfaithful to him. He had Scriptural grounds for divorce in each case. Therefore, he had a right to remarry according to the teaching of Jesus in Matthew 19:9. He met and married his fourth wife who was a good moral woman. In time they heard and obeyed the Gospel and became zealous workers in the kingdom. Paul's inspired warning needs to be repeated and heeded: "Do not be deceived; evil company corrupts good habits" (1 Corinthians 15:33).

Sixth, one will most likely marry someone he dates. Therefore, to be assured of marrying a Christian, it makes sense that one should only date those who are faithful Christians. There is no better place to meet your future marriage partner than at church or during a church related activity such as a camp, lectureship, Gospel meeting, or while attending a Christian college or university.

Seventh, one should always pray for the Lord's providential guidance in finding his future marriage partner. The Bible abundantly and clearly teaches that God hears and answers the prayers of His faithful children: "For the eyes of the Lord are on the righteous, and His ears are open to their prayers; but the face of the Lord is against those who do evil" (1 Peter 3:12). One who is seeking a husband or wife should pray daily to the Lord to bless him in this matter. In the fulness of time, his prayers will be answered (Matthew 7:7-11; Luke 18:1-8.).

Eighth, one must be prepared to live and make a living. Many young couples are in love and rush into marriage without any forethought about how they are to keep house, pay the bills, etc. Mothers would do well to make sure their daughters know how to make and keep a budget, shop for groceries, cook, clean house, do laundry, iron and all the many things that go into running a household. Paul admonished older women to "admonish the younger women to love their husbands, to love their children, to be discreet, chaste, homemakers, good, obedient to their own husbands, that the Word of God may not be blasphemed" (Titus 2:4,5).

Fathers need to teach their sons by precept and example how to treat their wives. They must also see that their sons are trained in a trade or profession by which they can earn a living. It is said that ancient Jewish fathers had a proverb: "He who does not teach his son a trade teaches him to be a thief." Perhaps this explains why the apostle Paul, a scholar in the Jewish law, was also trained in the trade of making tents. Paul wrote: "If anyone does not provide for his own, and especially for those of his household, he has denied the faith and is worse than an unbeliever" (1 Timothy 5:8).

Ninth, one must prepare for marriage by taking sufficient time for courtship. Dating is the time to get acquainted, to learn the likes and dislikes of one another, to see what you have in common, and to learn areas in which you are not in agreement. It is a time to discuss these matters. Dating should be more than just doing "fun things" together such as going to sports events, movies and parties. A lot of time ought to be spent in conversation. Couples who truly love one another will seldom lack something to talk about.

Dating is also the time to get acquainted with the family of the one who may become your future marriage partner. When one marries, he is not only marrying an individual, but he is marrying into a family with its commonly held beliefs, customs, traditions, ways of thinking, and outlook on the world. One's future marriage partner, having grown up in a particular family, will have imbibed their pride and prejudices, opinions and outlooks, traditions and idiosyncrasies.

Courtship, especially as the couple falls deeply in love and begins planning to marry, is the right time to discuss practical matters such as how they will handle their money, where they will live, how many children they plan to have and when, how they will make decisions in various areas, etc.

Extremely short courtships are very unwise. One should never rush into something as serious as marriage. A wise old proverb says: "Marry in haste; repent in leisure." On the other hand, extremely long courtships may be unwise also. When a couple is deeply in love, they may be tempted to engage in sexual relations before marriage. The apostle Paul warned of the danger of sexual immorality (fornication):

"Flee sexual immorality. Every sin that a man does is outside the body, but he who commits sexual immorality sins against his own body. Or do you not know that your body is the temple of the Holy Spirit who is in you, whom you have from God and you are not your own? For you were bought with a price; Therefore, glorify God in your body and in your spirit, which are God's" (1 Corinthians 6:18-20).

Tenth, it is usually wise to marry someone who has a similar background to yours. Fewer adjustments will need to be made for the couple to be compatible if they are from common backgrounds and therefore already have similar ways of thinking. Some of the areas of compatibility to consider are: (1) age; (2) race; (3) economic background; (4) level of education; (5) national background; (6) religious background. These are not listed in order of importance for all are important and may influence whether a marriage is happy and successful or is miserable and ends in divorce or desertion.

Marrying someone who is close in age is not mandatory but it is usually wise. Those who have lived long are aware of how one changes physically, mentally, and in likes and dislikes as he grows older. A twenty-five year old and a fifty year old may fall in love, but they may be miles apart in wisdom, maturity and physical ability. It is not wrong (sinful) to marry someone in a different age bracket, but doing so may require extra effort and patience to adjust and maintain compatibility.

Marrying one from a different race is certainly not sinful for God is the Creator of all mankind (Acts 17:26) and is no respecter of persons (Acts 10:34,35); neither should we be! No single race is superior or inferior to other races. Physically, mentally, spiritually and emotionally all races are essentially the same. Sadly, we live in a world where many are ignorant, proud or prejudiced. Because of this, racially mixed marriages may be more difficult for couples and especially for their children.

If a person marries one from a different economic background, he may have to adjust his standard of living. There may be difficulty in living on a lower economic scale if one has come from a wealthy family and married lower on the economic scale. One may find he does not even fit in socially with those on a higher economic level.

Education is another area where adjustment may be difficult. For instance, if one with a PhD. marries one who has only a high school education, the couple may find they have different interests and therefore have very little to talk about. One's educational background often influences how he looks at the world and which level of society he feels most comfortable in. It is not wrong to marry someone with less or greater education than one has, but most likely adjustments will have to be made.

If a man from one nation marries a woman from a different nation, or even if a couple each come from a different section of the same nation, there can be cultural differences as well as very different political views and variant ways of thinking and doing things. Each will have to make adjustments and common ground will have to be sought in order for the couple to be compatible and the marriage successful.

Major differences which require changes on the part of one or both persons usually come after the wedding when the honeymoon is over and the couple settles down to everyday life. National or sectional loyalties, different tastes in food, political views, and preferences in social activities may also cause problems.

Perhaps the most common difference in background which causes strife and even heartache in a marriage is when a dedicated Christian marries one who is of no religious faith or of a different faith. This will cause problems, not only for the couple, but also for their children. The situation is usually resolved in one of three ways: (1) One of the partners will convert to the religion of the other in order to keep peace in the family; (2) Both will give up religion altogether and simply live worldly, godless lives. In this case, the children are the losers; (3) Each will try to maintain his faith despite the opposition that may come from the other and the strife which often results.

The best solution is prevention. For one who is serious about serving God, the wise thing to do is to marry another of the same faith. It is very difficult for a strong Christian to be unable to share his faith with the one he loves most in this world. Christians, determine that you are not going to marry anyone unless he is a strong, faithful Christian. Begin to date only those who are fellow Christians. Participate in church activities that will put you in company with others of your age, interests, and dedication. Your marriage partner can do more to help you go to Heaven than anyone else. Conversely, he can do more to make it difficult for you to go to Heaven. However, a couple who are one in Christ and faithful to Him in every way can help one another go to Heaven.

As you prepare for marriage, make your decisions in the light of eternity. Marry only someone you believe will help you go to Heaven. Absolutely do not marry someone you feel could be a hindrance to your serving the Lord faithfully. Marry someone who will be the right teacher and best role model for your children and who will help them go to Heaven. Do not marry someone with whom you cannot share the most important thing in your life - your faith in Jesus Christ, the Son of God. Marry a faithful, dedicated Christian, a member of the Lord's church. You will be glad in this life and in the greater eternal life to come.

REVIEW QUESTIONS

1. If anyone desires to follow Jesus, who and what must he hate (in the sense of love less)?

2. Before undertaking important tasks in life, what should one do?

3. Name the two parables Jesus taught to show that we must count the cost if we want to be His disciple.

4. If one is planning to marry, what must he also do?

5. In the past as well as in some cultures still today, how does one find a marriage partner?

6. What is the first step in preparation for marriage?

7. If one is holy, what are some things he will strive to avoid?

8. Who are the only people who have a right to engage in sexual relations?

9. What was God's plan for marriage that He laid down in the beginning?

10. What is the one exception to this original plan that Jesus Himself gave?

11. Who are responsible for teaching our young people that marriage is a life long commitment that must not be entered into lightly?

12. Who is the most likely person one will marry?

13. Where is the best place to meet one's future marriage partner?

14. What should mothers teach their daughters in order to prepare them for marriage?

15. What should fathers teach their sons to prepare them for marriage?

16. Which is best? Extremely short engagements or extremely long ones?

17. In light of what should one make his decisions as he prepares for marriage?

18. Is it important to know the family of the one you intend to marry? Why?

Chapter 7: FAITHFUL FATHERS ARE INDISPENSABLE

A growing number of homes today have only one parent in them. The parent who is absent is most often the husband and father. There are several reasons fathers are disappearing from homes. Chief among them are (1) divorce; (2) desertion; (3) drug and alcohol addiction; (4) delinquency (men who father children out of wedlock and refuse to take responsibility for them); and (5) death, which is the only valid and acceptable reason for the permanent absence of fathers from the home.

Children who do not have a father or father figure in their home are at a great disadvantage. They are much more likely to live below the poverty level. They are also much more likely to drop out of school before graduation, thereby jeopardizing their entire future. In addition, they are at much higher risk of being in trouble with authorities at school and with the law of the land. The children who suffer the upheaval of their parents' marriage breakup will bear the scars for the remainder of their lives.

There is simply no substitute for the home as God planned it in the beginning with a man and woman who are committed to one another for life. This home has the husband and father as the head, protector and provider and the wife and mother as the manager of the home and caretaker and guide of the children. The children are taught by their parents to love, honor and obey them. No better arrangement for bringing children into the world, nurturing them, and raising God fearing, law abiding, useful members of society has ever been, nor can ever be devised.

Why is it so essential that fathers be in the home fulfilling their God-given responsibilities? Following are several reasons which are given in God's holy Book, the Bible. First, a husband and father is the head of his home according to God's plan. This is a very unpopular and politically incorrect view today, but it is God's own plan nevertheless. In fact, it has been God's will from the beginning and will remain His will until the end of the world.

Today, traditional marriage ceremonies, which include the bride promising to love, honor and obey her husband, are being discarded. The radical Feminist Movement considers marriages based upon the teaching of God's Word to be out of date and discriminatory against women. However, God's Word has not changed. Just as God made the woman as a helper comparable to man in the beginning, and created marriage for the mutual happiness of man and woman and the bearing and nurturing of children, God's basic laws governing marriage have not changed (Genesis 2:24; Matthew 19:4-6).

"Wives, submit to your own husbands, as to the Lord. For the husband is the head of the wife, as also Christ is the head of the church; and He is the Savior of the body. Therefore, just as the church is subject to Christ, so let the wives be to their own husbands in everything" (Ephesians 5:22-24; Colossians 3:18).

Second, husbands and fathers are charged with the responsibility of making a living for their family so that their essential needs for food, clothing, shelter, and education are met. The Bible teaches this responsibility:

> "But if anyone does not provide for his own, and especially for those of his household, he has denied the faith and is worse than an unbeliever" (1 Timothy 5:8).

Today, we have coined a new phrase in English to describe fathers of dependent children who shirk their responsibility to provide for their offspring. They are called (and rightly so) "deadbeat dads." Could there be anyone more worthy of the contempt and condemnation of right thinking and morally responsible people than a man who simply refuses to feed and clothe his own helpless and dependent children?!

Third, a home without a father in it is lacking an indispensable ingredient of a child's upbringing, which is a father to teach him about God and how to live to be pleasing to Him. Most children do not receive any spiritual training at all in the home. Those who do generally receive it from their mother. Godly mothers who take up the slack left by unbelieving or uncaring fathers deserve our commendation and gratitude. However, God squarely places the responsibility of training and admonition of children on the shoulders of fathers.

> "And you fathers, do not provoke your children to wrath, but bring them up in the training and admonition of the Lord" (Ephesians 6:4).

God has always required parents to teach His will to their children. Fathers, as the heads of their homes, must take the lead in the spiritual training of their children. This was God's will under the Law of Moses just as it is under the New Testament in the Christian Age. In the Law, God emphasized that the teaching of His will should be done naturally as occasion afforded opportunities:

> "Hear, O Israel: The Lord our God is One! You shall love the Lord your God with all your heart, with all your souls, and with all your strength. And these words which I command you today shall be in your heart. You shall teach them diligently to your children, and shall talk of them when you sit in your house, when you walk by the way, when you lie down, and when you rise up, You shall bind them as a sign on your hand, and they shall be as frontlets between your eyes. You shall write them on the doorposts of your house and on your gates" (Deuteronomy 6:4-9).

Fathers, do your children hear you give thanks to God before each meal? Do you have a family Bible study or devotional each day? Do you attend Bible study and worship at every opportunity and take your family with you? Do your children ever hear you and their mother discuss the Scriptures? Do you understand that worship and Bible study must always take priority over sports, concerts, recreation and other activities?

Do your children understand this? Have they come to learn the importance of worshiping God by the example you have set before them?

Fourth, a father must be a good example before his wife and their children. Paul told the young preacher, Timothy: "Let no one despise your youth, but be an example to the believers in word, in conduct, in love, in spirit, in faith, in purity" (1 Timothy 4:12). If it is necessary that a young preacher be an example in these areas, is not it even more important for a husband and father to be such an example before his own wife and children?

Husbands and fathers should so live that God may be able to say of them as He did of Abraham:

"For I know him, that he will command his children and his household after him, and they shall keep the way of the Lord, to do justice and judgment; that the Lord may bring upon Abraham that which He has spoken of him" (Genesis 18:19; KJV).

The importance of a father's example cannot be too greatly emphasized. A father received a Father's Day gift from his teenage son. The gift was a useful book but the inscription written in it by his son made the book invaluable, a treasure, to his father. Inscribed were these words: "Dad, you're the greatest! I am very proud of you. I hope to be just like you someday!"

An unknown poet penned the following meaningful verse:

"There are little eyes watching you every night and day:
There are little ears that listen to everything you say'
There are little hands all eager to do everything you do;
There are little ones dreaming of being just like you!"

Fifth, a father needs to be present in the home. How can he fulfill his duties otherwise? He may have to work long hours at times to earn a living for his family. However, a busy father must make time to be with his wife and children. They need to spend time with him and he with them. A father needs to wrestle and play ball with his sons and have tea parties and play games or read to his daughters. He needs to attend their school activities such as open house, school plays, recitals, ball games and other sporting events. In short, he must be a "hands on Dad."

Children grow up fast. Many parents have said at their child's graduation or wedding, "How did this happen so fast? It seems only yesterday that he (or she) was just a baby or just starting school?" Many parents have realized only too late that they have missed out on many wonderful moments in life by not being there when these memorable moments occurred.

Sixth, a good father is faithful to the mother of his children. As head of his home, a husband must "love his wife just as Christ loved the church and gave Himself for her" (Ephesians 5:25). How much did Christ love His church? Enough to die for it. During His earthly ministry, He taught His apostles that "greater love hath no man than this, that a man lay down his life for his friends" (John 15:13; KJV). However, He showed an even greater love than this, for He died not only for His friends, but also for His enemies, even those who crucified Him.

> "For when we were still without strength, in due time Christ died for the ungodly. For scarcely for a righteous man will one die, yet perhaps for a good man someone would even dare to die. But God demonstrates His own love toward us, in that while we were still sinners, Christ died for us" (Romans 5:6-8).

If a husband truly loves his wife, he will gladly die to save her should the necessity arise. Several years ago, a news story told of a home invasion by a drug addict who was high on drugs and desperately seeking money for another "fix." He broke into the home of an elderly couple who were enjoying a quiet evening at home. The husband was a retired, much decorated military officer. The addict pointed a gun at the man's wife and screamed that he would pull the trigger if the man did not give him money immediately. The husband instinctively stepped in front of his wife to protect her. The addict pulled the trigger killing him instantly. He fled the scene of the crime and was later apprehended by the police. The husband truly loved his wife and demonstrated it by giving his life to save her life.

Children need the security of knowing their parents are devoted and dedicated to one another. When fathers and mothers fight, whether it is verbal or physical, their children are frightened and insecure. When their parents are kind, gentle, patient and loving with one another, nothing gives their children greater happiness and peace.

Seventh, a father as head of his home must accept his role as the authority figure in the home. This means he will take the lead in disciplining his children when the need arises. Discipline is teaching and training in right living. It includes punishment for disobedience and wrong behavior. This teaches a child the lesson that if he does wrong, there is a price to be paid. Just as the laws of the land are worthless if they are not enforced and suitable punishment meted out for violating them, the same is true in principle in the home. If children do not learn at home that misbehavior will be punished, they will have very unhappy and unfulfilled lives. They will get into trouble at school. They will find it hard to keep a job and carry out an employer's instructions. They most likely will not respect the laws of the land either and may soon find themselves in trouble with law enforcement officials.

The inspired writer of the book of Hebrews encouraged Christians to remain steadfast in the faith even though persecution would come. However, not all suffering or persecution is bad for God can use it to make us stronger. The inspired writer then quoted from the Old Testament book of Proverbs to show how God uses trials to discipline His children to make them stronger.

"And you have forgotten the exhortation which speaks to you as to sons: 'My son, do not despise the chastening of the Lord, nor be discouraged when you are rebuked by Him; for whom the Lord loves He chastens, and scourges every son whom He receives.' If you endure chastening, God deals with you as with sons; for what son is there whom a father does not chasten? But if you are without chastening of which all have become partakers, then you are illegitimate and not sons. Furthermore, we have had human fathers who corrected us, and we paid them respect. Shall we not much more readily be in subjection to the Father of spirits and live? For they indeed for a few days chastened us as seemed best to them, but He for our profit that we may become partakers of His holiness. Now no chastening seems for the present to be joyful, but painful; but afterward it bears the peaceable fruit of righteousness to those who have been trained by it" (Hebrews 12:5-11).

Eighth, fathers must truly be Christians if they want their children to have the blessings of Christ in this life and eternal joy in the life to come. An elderly Christian man with tears in his eyes confessed, "I was not a faithful Christian when my children were growing up. I lived in the world and set a bad example before them. I have repented and returned to the Lord in my old age, but my son, because of my bad example, remains in the world."

One may be an acceptable, even a good father, as the world considers it, while living outside of Christ. However, he cannot be the best kind of father for he is depriving his children of a father whose teaching and example they can trust to lead them in the way to eternal life. Dear Reader, if you have not truly dedicated yourself to Christ by obeying His Gospel and living as He directs, you need to change! You must change, not only for the sake of your own eternal salvation, but also for the salvation of your children. Do not be the example that leads your children to Hell!

To become a Christian one must hear the Gospel of Jesus Christ "who died for our sins according to the Scriptures, was buried, and arose again the third day according to the Scriptures" (1 Corinthians 15:1-4). Having heard, one must believe in Jesus Christ as God's Son who died for him (John 3:16; 8:24). Faith comes by hearing the Word of God (Romans 10:17). Having heard and believed in Jesus the Christ, one will repent of all his past sins (Luke 13:3; Acts 2:38; 2 Corinthians 7:10). Repentance is a change of one's mind toward sin. It is brought about by godly sorrow for having sinned again God, and it results in a change of life. One will then want to confess his faith in Christ before men "for with the heart man believes unto righteousness, and with the mouth confession is made unto salvation" (Romans 10:10; Acts 8:37, KJV). Then one will be baptized (immersed in water) in the name of Jesus Christ for the remission (forgiveness) of sins (Mark 16:15,16; Acts 2:38; 22:16; Romans 6:1-18; Galatians 3:26,27).

By obedience to the Gospel, one is "born again of water and the Spirit" (John 3:3-5); he is added by the Lord to His church (Acts 2:41; 47); he has died to sin and risen to "walk in newness of life" (Romans 6:3,4). He is therefore a "new creation" (2 Corinthians 5:17). He has "clothed himself with Christ" and is "in Christ" (Galatians 3:27). He now has the promise and hope of eternal life (1 John 2:25; Titus 1:2). As a Christian father, he will be able to teach, lead and guide his children in "the strait and narrow way which leads to eternal life" by his teaching, example and counsel (Matthew 7:13,14). He can have the confident expectation of being with his wife and children in Heaven through the endless ages. There is no greater blessing, gift, or riches than this!!

We conclude this chapter with a statement which summarizes the character of one who is truly a Christian father:

"The father in the home is the cornerstone of discipline, the strength of love, and the example to emulate. To be a truly great Christian father, one must be the right kind of man. A father, in being the right kind of man, must bear responsibility, bear up under adversity and seek the spiritual welfare of each member of the family including himself. A father must be a gentleman always. He must not be guilty of violence, sensuality, and greed lest he lose his soul and the souls of those entrusted to his care. To be a great father and of great value, he must be like God" (Andrew Connally: Spiritual Sword; April 1984).

REVIEW QUESTIONS

1. Which parent is most often missing from today's homes?

2. List five reasons fathers are disappearing from today's homes.

3. What are some of the risks faced by children who come from homes without a father present in it?

4. According to God's plan, who is the head of the home? Give Scripture.

5. What is the promise that brides traditionally made that is often left out of modern marriage ceremonies?

6. How does the Feminist Movement regard marriage based upon the teaching of the Bible?

7. What are fathers called who do not support their dependent children?

8. What is an indispensable ingredient for children's upbringing?

9. Where does God squarely place the responsibility for training and admonishing children to bring them up in the Lord's way?

10. Of whom did the Lord say, "For I know him that he will command his children and his household after him"?

11. How much must a husband love his wife according to Ephesians 5:25?

12. How do children feel when their parents fight?

13. If a father is not a Christian, of what is he depriving his children?

14. What kind of a man must one be in order to be a truly great Christian father?

15. What does Paul say about a man who does not provide for his own family and household?

16. What is discipline? What does it include?

17. If one is without chastening by his father, what kind of son is he?

18. What must one do to become a true Christian?

Chapter 8:   GODLY MOTHERS ARE A MUST!

It has been frequently said that the most beautiful words in any language are "home" and "mother." The two words go together for it is hard to think of one without the other. Home has a special place in our hearts because our mothers are there, if not in reality for some have passed away, but in our fondest memories.

There was a time not so long ago when most homes were stable. Divorce and remarriage were uncommon and frowned upon by respectable members of the community. Abortion was nearly unheard of and was illegal. Same sex marriages and relationships were illegal and viewed with abhorrence by most people. Living together without the commitment of marriage was contemptuously called "shacking up." It was universally regarded as sinful, shameful, and disgraceful. Husbands and fathers earned the living to support their wives and children. Mother and wives were proud to stay in the home, keep the house and raise their children.

This began to change in the 1940's during the Second World War. While husbands were away fighting on the far flung battlefields of the world, wives and mothers were leaving their homes and going to work in factories producing materials for the war effort. Women began to fill jobs that formerly were done only by men. When the war was over, many of them continued to work in business and industry. Prior to this time if women held jobs outside the home it was usually as secretaries, teachers, nurses, or clerks. Women began to seek higher education or specialized training and joined men in the professions as business executives, doctors, lawyers, dentists, scientists, architects, professors, etc.

The result of women working full-time jobs was that families became dependent upon having two household incomes and increased their standard of living accordingly. Married couples began having fewer children. Their children were raised in daycare centers or by babysitters. Children spent less and less time with their parents and became more involved in outside activities such as sports, music, ballet, martial arts, etc.

Families no longer gathered around the dinner table in the evenings to share the experiences of their day. Instead, they ate "fast food" or "TV dinners" in front of the television. Family life and relationships declined. Present day families are not as close as families once were. They do fewer things together as a family. Often husbands and wives work different hours at their jobs. They seldom see each other during the day and at times may barely see one another for several days. The amount of personal time parents spend with their children is less now than ever before in human history. This has brought about numerous problems.

Children often come home from school to an empty house for both parents are still at work. These "latch key kids," as they have come to be known, may be alone for hours before the parents come home. It is not unusual for them to be injured or get into trouble when they are home alone without adult supervision.

The present day radical feminist movement has added to the confusion. They often belittle women who choose to stay at home and raise their children. Feminists look down upon them thinking they are wasting their time and talents and must be unfulfilled. A woman who follows the Scriptures and is in submission to her husband is ridiculed and considered little better than a slave to him and to their children.

Many modern daycare centers are well run but professionals are seldom as careful and concerned as actual parents, especially mothers. Christian mothers who want their children brought up with Christian teaching may find their children are taking on a very different world view than their own. This is only intensified when children enter the public school system and study under teachers whose education in public schools and universities has thoroughly indoctrinated them in humanism, agnosticism, evolution, socialism, and many other worldly philosophies which are diametrically opposed to the teachings of God's Book, the Bible. When our teenage children rebel and engage in worldly behavior, it is the natural outcome of the gradual but steady indoctrination they have received from their caretakers and teachers since infancy.

In a thoughtful book on the decline of Christian homes, Jim Nelson Black wrote:

"Today we have a generation of children growing up 'unbonded' ... children growing up with no sense of relationship or responsibility to other people. They have no allegiance to parents, no loyalty to friends, no concept of right and wrong, and they become social misfits and ultimately a menace to society.... ' They grow up in 'warehouses for kids' while their parents are somewhere else, trying to keep up a 'lifestyle!" (Jim Nelson Black: When Nations Die, pp. 220, 221).

What is the solution to this unhealthy and dangerous situation? There is only one answer. We must return to God's plan for the home, and that plan has mother in the home! Let us consider what God says in the Scriptures. The Bible teaches first of all that a wife will submit to her husband and obey him (Genesis 3:16; Ephesians 5:22-24; 1 Peter 3:1-6). She will love her husband and children. When she becomes older, she will teach young women to "love their husbands, to love their children, to be discreet, chaste, homemakers, good, obedient to their own husbands, that the Word of God may not blasphemed" (Titus 2:3-5).

The Greek word "oikourous" which is translated as "keepers at home "in the King James Version, is rendered as "homemakers" in the New King James Version. Strong's Exhaustive Concordance of the Bible defines it as "a stayer at home, i.e.. domestically inclined (a good housekeeper): - keeper at home." Thayer's Greek-English Lexicon of the New Testament defines "oikouros" as it is used in Titus 2:5 as "keeping at home and taking care of household affairs, domestic."

In his commentary on Paul's letters to Timothy and Titus, Wayne Jackson comments:

"Christian women who have children, and who farm them out to daycare centers and babysitters, simply because they desire a much more profitable lifestyle than they otherwise might have, have little, if any, understanding of the role of wife and mother. Many 'exegetes' have so busied themselves with what this passage does not mean they have concluded it means nothing" (Before I Die: Paul's Letters to Timothy and Titus: Christian Courier Publications; Stockton, California; 2007).

The Scriptures teach that younger widows should marry again and raise a family instead of being cared for by the church:

"Therefore, I desire that the younger widows marry, bear children, manage the house, give no opportunity to the adversary to speak reproachfully" (1 Timothy 5:14).

The phrase "manage the house" in the New King James Version is translated as "guide the house" in the King James Version (1611). George Ricker Berry's Interlinear Literal Translation of the Greek New Testament renders this phrase "to rule the house." Again, we see that a wife's domain is the home where as wife and mother, she reigns as queen.

Finally, regarding woman's God-given role, we must look briefly at 1 Timothy, chapter two. In this chapter, Paul is giving directive regarding the respective roles of men and women in the public worship of the church. Beginning in verse 9, he teaches that women, rather than taking a public leadership role, should adorn themselves modestly in such a way as not to draw attention to themselves. They are told to "learn in silence with all submission." He further wrote: "And I do not permit a woman to teach or to have authority over a man, but to be in silence." The word for silence in the original is "hesuchios" which does not mean absolute silence but rather quietness according to W. E. Vine in An Expository Dictionary of New Testament Words.

In the verses which follow, Paul states two reasons that women are not to have dominion over man by teaching or taking public leadership in the worship: (1) Adam was formed first and woman made for him and from him (Genesis 2:18-25); (2) Adam was not deceived, but the woman being deceived led in the transgression (Genesis 3:1-6;16). This command has nothing to do with culture but rather order of creation and the woman being deceived in the transgression. Paul then makes a statement lest women fall into despair:

"Nevertheless she will be saved in childbearing if they continue in faith, love, and holiness, with self control" (verse 15).

God has made man the leader in public teaching and worship. Woman is forbidden to take this role because the man was first in creation and woman led in the fall into sin in the Garden of Eden. However, that women be not discouraged, Paul points out that they can and will be saved: "...she will be saved in childbearing."

God is not saying that women must have children in order to be saved. This would condemn unmarried women as well as married women who cannot have children. Neither is God saying that the mere fact of a woman bearing children will guarantee her admission into Heaven. He is saying that women are created to be wives and mothers and it will be by means of their faithfully fulfilling their unique role in their natural domain, that of the home, as a wife and mother, that women will find salvation provided they faithfully live the Christian life.

Why should woman desire the leadership role in the church that God gave to men? Just as man cannot take woman's place in the home, woman cannot take man's place in the church that God has ordained for him. The continuation of the human race depends upon women. The difference between civilization and chaos is largely influenced by women. It is an old, but still true statement that "the hand that rocks the cradle rules the world." Mothers have the greatest opportunity to influence the very future of nations for they mold and make the children who will grow into the future leaders. President Abraham Lincoln well understood this when he stated, "All that I am and have I owe to my angel mother."

The beautiful description of the worthy woman (or virtuous wife) whose price is far above rubies is found in Proverbs 31:10-31. It is a picture of the ideal woman from an Old Testament prospective. It was originally written to God's Old Testament people, Israel, but has relevance for us today (Romans 15:4). After warning about immoral women who entice men to commit adultery (Proverbs 2:16-19; 5:15-20; 6:23-35; 7:4-27), women who lack discretion (11:22) and contentious, angry, nagging wives (21:9,19; 25:24), Proverbs ends in an ascription of praise to the highest ideal of womanhood to be found in the entire Old Testament.

The virtuous wife (NKJV) of Proverbs 31:10-31 is shown to be a multi-talented, multi-tasking wife and mother. Far from being inept, lazy, unintelligent, or inefficient as feminists like to portray stay at home mothers, this woman is godly, hard-working, kind, and very capable. The demands of being a Christian wife and mother and doing it well are great. A woman who takes on this work will wear many "hats." She must be a housekeeper, cook, babysitter, nurse, teacher, shopper for family food, needs and supplies, keeper of household finances, secretary, teacher, her husband's loving companion, gracious hostess to guests, playmate to her children, etc. Let us note some of the many beautiful attributes of the virtuous wife:

The virtuous wife is a faithful and diligent helper to her husband:

"The heart of her husband safely trusts her; so he will have no lack of gain.
She does him good and not evil all the days of her life" (verses 11,12).

The virtuous wife is a wise businesswoman:

"She considers a field and buys it; from her profits she plants a vineyard" (v. 16).

45

Please note that she bought a field and planted a vineyard. Families in Israel often had vineyards for their own food sources. She did not open a real estate office and compete in the business world. Her business activities are home centered.

The virtuous wife is not lazy. She is diligent in her duties and works hard.

"She also rises while it is yet night, and provides food for her household, and a portion for her maidservants" (verse 15).

The virtuous woman is benevolent and concerned about the poor:

"She extends her hands to the poor; yes, she reaches out her hand to the needy" (verse 20).

The virtuous woman demonstrates the truthfulness of the old saying: "Behind every great man is a great woman." She contributes to her husband's success and standing in the community. She is not ashamed of him or jealous of his success but shows her support standing by his side.

"Her husband is known in the gates when he sits among the elders of the land" (verse 23).

The virtuous wife is both wise and kind in her dealings with others:

"Strength and honor are her clothing; she shall rejoice in time to come. She opens her mouth with wisdom and on her tongue is the law of kindness" (verses 25,26).

The virtuous wife is loved and highly esteemed by her husband and children.

"Her children rise up and call her blessed; her husband also, and he praises her" (verse 28).

The virtuous wife possesses true and lasting beauty:

"Charm is deceitful and beauty is passing, but a woman who fears the Lord, she shall be praised" (verse 30).

To summarize the great and essential position of women in their God-given roles as wives and mothers, we add the following important places they fill: they teach other women and children; they assist their husbands in teaching men just as Priscilla assisted Aquila in Acts 18; they counsel and encourage younger women; they "let their lights shine" and set proper examples for Christian women and girls to follow; they minister to the sick by cooking, cleaning and caring for them; they encourage their husbands to be men of God and stand behind them in their responsibilities without dictating to them; they prepare their daughters to be Christian wives and mothers; they serve quietly behind the scenes in many ways performing services that will not be known until Judgment Day. On that great Day, the Lord will say to them, "Come, you blessed of My Father, inherit the kingdom prepared for you from the foundation of the world" (Matthew 25:34).

The question is sometimes asked, "What about women who are widows, or whose husbands have deserted them, or their children are grown and on their own? Is it wrong for such mothers to seek employment outside the home?" There are cases where mothers must leave the home to seek employment if no other source of income is available. If one's children are grown and on their own, certainly a mother does not have the responsibility in the home that she had when the children were young and dependent. When necessity demands, a mother may have to seek work outside the home to support her family. Some wives and mothers, like the virtuous wife in Proverbs 31, have engaged in gainful employment from the home. For example, one mother took care of small children in her home in order that she might be at home with her own children. In this way, she brought in extra income and also had an influence for good on the children she cared for through the years. This does not alter the fact that the Bible teaches that wives and mothers are to be keepers at home. There are many dangers when mothers turn their children over to others to raise who do not share their Christian values.

R.C Marshall in <u>Memories of Home and Happiness</u> described the integral role of his mother in his home when he was growing up in the early twentieth century:

"She was always there for us. She prepared a hot breakfast for us every morning and saw we were ready for school. She assigned us chores when we came home from school and made us do our homework. She always had a hot, nourishing meal on the table every evening that we ate together as a family. She washed, ironed, and mended our clothes. She baked our birthday cakes and made cookies for us when we came home from school. She taught us to read the Bible and pray and took us to Sunday school and worship every week. She loved and respected our Dad and taught us to do the same. She hugged us when we were sad, tended our cuts and bruises when we fell or got hurt, and kept a vigil at our bedside when we were sick. She was our confidant and counselor as we grew older. She welcomed our spouses when we married and delighted in our children. Mom was always there, in good times and bad. She was a stable factor in our lives. We could always count on her!"

REVIEW QUESTIONS

1. Which two words are said to be the most beautiful words in any language?

2. Why does home have a special place in our hearts?

3. What is "shacking up?" Is it approved by God?

4. What event caused women to begin doing jobs that formerly had been done by men?

5. What are "latch key" children?

6. How do feminists regard women who chose to be full-time wives and mothers rather than pursue a career?

7. What are "unbonded" children? What causes children to be "unbonded?"

8. What does Paul tell young widows they should do rather than rely on support from the church?

9. If women are forbidden by God to be leaders in the church, how can they be saved?

10. To whom did President Abraham Lincoln give credit for all he had achieved in life?

11. Are the roles of men and women in the church simply matters of culture, or are they based on the order of creation and the fall in the Garden of Eden?

12. What are some of the various "hats" homemakers must wear?

13. Where in the Old Testament do we read of "the virtuous wife?"

14. Must a woman give birth to children in order to go to Heaven?

15. What is the meaning of the statement regarding woman: "Nevertheless, she shall be saved in childbearing?"

16. What causes teenage children who have grown up in Christian homes to engage in worldly behavior?

17. Are families today as close as they were before World War II? Why or why not?

Chapter 9:   CHILDREN ARE A HERITAGE FROM THE LORD (1)

From the beginning of the world, children have been regarded as a blessing from God. It is only in recent times in our affluent and self-centered society that children are no longer valued as they once were. The Psalmist praised God for the blessings that children bring.

"Behold, children are a heritage from the Lord; the fruit of the womb is a reward. Like arrows in the hand of a warrior, so are the children of one's youth. Happy is the man who has his quiver full of them; they shall not be ashamed, but shall speak with their enemies in the gate" (Psalm 127:3-5).

In the beginning, God commanded men and women to "Be fruitful and multiply; and fill the earth and subdue it" (Genesis 1:28). Marriage is the institution by which children are safely brought into the world with a father to provide for and protect them and a mother to care for and nurture them. Man cannot improve upon God's plan! Efforts to change or bypass it have always proved disastrous!

Not long after Adam and Eve were driven from the Garden of Eden, the Bible records:

"Now Adam knew Eve his wife, and she conceived and bore Cain, and said, 'I have acquired a man from the Lord.' Then she bore again, this time his brother Abel" (Genesis 4:1,2).

After Cain killed Abel, the Divine Record states:

"And Adam knew his wife again, and she bore a son and named him Seth, 'For God has appointed another seed for me instead of Abel, whom Cain killed'" (Genesis 4:25).

Following the birth of Seth, the Scriptures summarize, saying of Adam: "… he had sons and daughters" (Genesis 5:4).

The men and women whose illustrious lives are recorded in Sacred Scripture truly considered children to be a gift from God. Sarah, wife of Abraham, was barren. They were not blessed with children until old age when Sarah was beyond the age of child-bearing and Abraham was past the normal age of begetting children. God had promised them a son and they waited patiently for many years. When the time was right, God gave them Isaac (Genesis 15:1-21:7; Romans 4:13-22).

Isaac married Rebekah. Twenty years passed and they had no children. The Bible says:

"Now Isaac pleaded with the Lord for his wife because she was barren; and the Lord granted his plea, and Rebekah, his wife, conceived" (Genesis 25:21).

In the days of the Judges, a righteous woman named Hannah, the wife of Elkanah, had no children. She was greatly grieved at her sad condition. When her family made their annual pilgrimage to Shiloh where the tabernacle was located in those days, Hannah "prayed to the Lord and wept in anguish." She promised the Lord that if He gave her a son, she would dedicate him to the Lord's service all the days of his life. God heard her prayer. A son was born to Hannah and Elkanah and they named him Samuel. Samuel became the last and perhaps the greatest of the judges of Israel (1 Samuel 1:1-4:1).

In the New Testament, we learn of a godly couple, Zacharias and Elizabeth, who were old and had no children for Elizabeth was barren. Zacharias prayed to God for a son. God in His own time answered the prayer of Zacharias. A son was born to them late in life. They named him "John" as an angel had commanded (Luke 1). John became known as "John the Immerser" when he was grown. He was a great preacher whose coming was prophesied in the Old Testament as the one who would prepare a people for the coming of the Christ (Isaiah 40:3; Malachi 3:1;4:5,6; Mark 1:1-13).

Sadly, many today, instead of desiring to have children, do not want children. They place their career, love of money, or social standing ahead of raising a family. Too many of today's married couples prefer their pets to children. Dogs and other pets receive the affection and attention that parents once lavished upon their children. Some older people who would love to have grandchildren have been heard to say, "I don't have any grandchildren. I have grand-dogs." Pets, whether dogs or other animals, can provide company for people living alone. There is nothing wrong with one having pets and enjoying them, but they must never take the place of children. Will our pets care for us when we are old? Many young couples who have chosen not to have children will one day regret their decision when they are elderly and have no one to care for them.

Some couples are unable to have children even though they greatly desire them. Many of them have chosen to adopt orphans who long to have a good, stable home with parents who love them. This is a good work which receives the approval and commendation of God and brings joy to the adoptive parents (Psalm 146:9; James 1:27).

One of the greatest tragedies of all time is not the loss of countless children to disease, starvation or the ravages of war, tragic though these are. The greatest tragedy of our modern world is the premeditated killing of untold millions of unborn infants in their mother's womb. Parents, with the sanction of society and the blessing of our federal government, perpetrate and condone this unspeakable atrocity! Since the United States Supreme Court handed down the Roe v. Wade decision in 1973, more than sixty million (60,000,000) precious babies made in God's image have been brutally torn from the womb by medical doctors who have hypocritically sworn to save lives, not take them. Millions of others, including some professed Christians, have stood idly by and allowed this shameful genocide to take place without so much as uttering a simple protest. Others, unthinking, continue to vote for candidates for public office and support political parties who advocate this mass killing of the innocent unborn. Do not be deceived! There will be a day of reckoning when the God of love and justice will punish those who are involved in such a heinous sin (Acts 17:30,31; 2 Corinthians 5:10).

The Bible says that God hates evil. Please note the words of the wise man:

"These six things the Lord hates,
Yes, seven are an abomination to Him;
A proud look, a lying tongue,
HANDS THAT SHED INNOCENT BLOOD,
A heart that devises wicked plans,
Feet that are swift in running to evil,
A false witness who speaks lies,
And one who sows discord among brethren"
(Proverbs 6:16-19).

What about those of us who have chosen to have children? Are we doing what God wants us to do to raise faithful, obedient, God-fearing children? Or, are the children we raise indistinguishable from the children of worldly parents? There is nothing in life that a couple can accomplish that is more useful to society, and more of a blessing to the parents, than raising children who are faithful to God, obedient to their parents and a blessing to society. Some years ago, a Christian counselor and author was frequently criticized because he and his wife had eight fine children. The critics pointed to the "overpopulation of the world and the shortage of vital services" and blamed parents of large families. The counselor simply replied to his critics, "The world needs more of the kind of children my wife and I are raising!"

Noah preached for one hundred and twenty years and made only seven converts, his wife, his three sons and their wives (1 Peter 3:18-20; 2 Peter 2:4,5; Genesis 6:3; 7:1,13). No man is truly a success in life whose family is lost to the world. Neither is a man a failure who has saved his family by teaching them the Word of God and living a righteous life before them.

A major concern of Christian parents and the leaders of the church in recent years has been the departure of many of our young people. They have left the Lord's church to go to the world or to join cults and sects formed by man. Parents often ask, "What did I do wrong? I took them to church every time the doors were open." Today, it takes much more than regular attendance at church services, although this is essential (Hebrews 10:25).

An article appeared in a Christian periodical several years ago. The author of the article asked a question: "Why is the church losing its young people?" He then answered his own question saying: "The church is not losing its young people! The home is!" Youth ministers and special programs for young people have not stopped the loss of many of our youth, although doubtless they have done much good. Until we return to God's plan for the home, we will continue to lose our children to man-made religions as well as to the world.

There are a number of things Christian parents fail to do which results in our children leaving the church. First, we too often set a poor example before our children. We criticize the preacher, elders, and deacons constantly and sometimes unmercifully. What kind of signal does this send to our children? Will they not come to regard the leadership of the church with lack of respect?

Second, we allow many activities such as school events, sports, and other activities to take precedence over Bible study and worship. This should never be! We must instill in our children by our teaching and example that we truly "seek first the kingdom of God and His righteousness" (Matthew 6:33). We must never miss Bible study or worship for worldly activities.

Third, we spend a great deal of money to insure that our children have the best secular education possible so they can succeed in business or professions in this brief life on earth. However, we give little thought or time to their eternal destiny when this short life on earth is over. Jesus asked: "For what profit is it to a man if he gains the whole world, and loses his own soul? Or what will a man give in exchange for his soul?" (Matthew 16:26).

Fourth, we emphasize worldly goals and activities above spiritual things. Too often our emphasis is on good grades in school, achievement in sports, the latest fashion in clothes, cars, money, popularity among one's peers, prestige, power, etc. John, the disciple whom Jesus loved, warned:

"Do not love the world or the things in the world. If anyone loves the world, the love of the Father is not in him. For all that is in the world - the lust of the flesh, the lust of the eyes, and the pride of life - is not of the Father but is of the world. And the world is passing away, and the lust of it; but he who does the will of God abides forever" (1 John 2:15-17).

Fifth, we permit our children to listen to music that uses vile language, promotes godless practices such as rebellion against authority, abortion, drugs, suicide, sex outside of marriage, euthanasia, drunkenness, etc. We do not supervise or even try to find out what our children are watching on television or viewing on their computers, or saying on social media, etc. We must teach them to "Keep your heart with all diligence, for out of it spring the issues of life" (Proverbs 4:23).

Sixth, we send our children to public schools from kindergarten to university, where they study under teachers who have been indoctrinated in humanism, evolution, atheism, agnosticism, socialism, relativism, situation ethics, and other godless philosophies. Why should we be surprised when they tell us they don't believe in God, Christ or the Bible anymore and refuse to go to church?

Seventh, we allow our children to dress like the world, wear the same immodest, indecent, revealing clothing, go to dances, participate in mixed swimming, and go to parties where responsible adult supervision is lacking and drugs and alcohol are available. We permit them to run around with worldly friends rather than seek their closest ties among Christians. Is it any wonder they leave the church for the world?

We live in this world, but we must not be of this world. Our citizenship is in Heaven (Philippians 3:20,21). We must teach our children to "set your mind on things above, not on things on the earth" (Colossians 3:2). And we must always be careful to model the right kind of behavior before our children. They are more likely to follow what we do than what we say.

More and more Christian parents are turning to homeschooling as an alternate to the public schools. There are many advantages to homeschooling for those who are serious about going to Heaven and educating their children for eternity.

First, homeschooling is done by the parents. Usually the mother bears the burden of the responsibility because the father in the family is working to earn a living. As parents, you can know exactly what is being taught. You can insure your children learn the truth not only in the Bible, but in science, history and other disciplines.

Second, your children are in a protected home environment. Not only are they safe from worldly, harmful teaching, but they are much safer physically than they would be in many public schools where bullying and other violence often take place.

Third, your children will get more personal attention and help than they can possibly get in most overcrowded public schools.

Fourth, you won't have to "unteach" your children things they learned in school as often concerned Christian parents have to when their children are in public schools.

Fifth, your children will do better overall academically than children in public schools. Testing in many states show that homeschooled children do as well and often better than their contemporaries in public schools.

Sixth, homeschooling provides greater flexibility. Therefore, parents have the flexibility to take their children to Bible lectureships, Christian camps, and other activities that would not be possible if they were in public schools.

Seventh, you can teach every course from the perspective of the Christian worldview. You also have the freedom of including a daily Bible and devotional period such as private Christian schools offer.

Eighth, parents who homeschool in a town or city may choose to meet once a month for children to have sports, art, music or language classes together.

REVIEW QUESTIONS

1. What was God's command given to men and women in the beginning?

2. How did men and women in Bible times regard having children?

3. Give some Bible examples of men and women who greatly desired to have children and asked God to bless them in this regard?

4. What do many modern couples place ahead of having children?

5. What do many older people long for, but do not have?

6. What is the greatest tragedy of modern times in regard to children?

7. Since 1973, how many in the United States of America have been legally killed in the womb of their mother?

8. What does God think about hands that shed innocent blood?

9. What is the greatest, most useful accomplishment that married couples can make to society?

10. Who is responsible for so many young people leaving the church? Is it the home or is it the church?

11. List some of the failures of parents which result in many young people leaving the church.

12. Are there any dangers in sending our children to public schools today? What are they?

13. Where are more and more parents turning as an alternative to sending their children to public schools?

14. List the advantages of homeschooling your children compared to sending them to the public schools?

15. Discussion Question: Are there any disadvantages to homeschooling? If so, what are they? If they exist, how can they be overcome?

16. What is one thing pets cannot do for us when we get old, but children can?

Chapter 10:   CHILDREN ARE A HERITAGE FROM THE LORD (2)

Parents have a responsibility to train their children to be accountable. The primary responsibility of parents in this life must be to save the souls of their children. The right kind of training will remain with your children throughout their lives. Fathers and mothers must begin training their child when he is young and impressionable. We need to teach our children the difference between right and wrong. We also need to teach them the difference between serving God and serving the Devil. They must come to understand the difference between worldly riches and the true riches which come from serving God. They must also learn the difference between Heaven and Hell and desire the former while shunning the latter.

In Ephesians 6:4, Paul warned fathers that they must not "…provoke your children to wrath." In other words, fathers must not make unreasonable demands of their children. It is possible for parents to be so unreasonably strict on their children that they drive them away from God (Colossians 3:21). Children should always be treated with fairness and kindness.

Children should be taught responsibility in the home. They should be assigned duties suitable for their age and ability. Having daily chores to do not only teaches a child to be responsible but helps him to realize nothing is free in life; that someone has to work to provide everything he has. Good duties to assign children according to age are simple jobs such as helping with the cleaning, taking the trash out, loading the dishwasher, clearing the table after a meal, mowing the grass, weeding the garden, making their own beds and keeping their rooms tidy. Not only do children learn responsibility, but such duties prepare them for caring for their own homes when they are grown.

Parents are especially responsible for the spiritual training of their children. This should be their number one priority! Jesus said: "Seek first the kingdom of God and His righteousness, and all these things (necessities of life) shall be added to you" (Matthew 6:33). The spiritual training of our children must be done by example as well as by direct instruction. Do you set a good example before your children? Do you always practice "the Golden Rule" (Matthew 7:12)? Do your children see you missing services of the church when you do not have a valid reason for doing so? Does your speech glorify God or take His Name in vain? Do your children see you treat their mother or father kindly? Do they observe you losing your temper easily and often? Are you grouchy, irritable and hard to get along with? Do your children see you pray and read the Bible?

In the Scriptures we read of a young man named Timothy. He is first mentioned in Acts 16:1-3. Paul saw the potential of this fine young man and wanted to train him to preach the Gospel. Timothy's father was a Gentile and probably an unbeliever, but the Scriptures specifically say his mother was a Jewess who believed. Paul trained Timothy who became an effective leader in the early church. Two letters of the New Testament were written specifically to him. In Second Timothy, chapter one, Paul remembers the genuine faith possessed by both Timothy's mother and grandmother (verse 5). In chapter 3, verse 15, Paul reminds Timothy that "… from childhood you have known the Holy Scriptures which are able to make you wise for salvation through faith which is in Christ Jesus." The church today needs young men who are grounded in God's Word and know how to proclaim it effectively. The best training begins in the home!

How much time do you spend with your children every day teaching them God's Word? First, we must take time every day with the exceptions of Sundays and Wednesdays when we take our children to Bible study. Have a set time and let nothing short of an emergency interfere with it. There are various ways to teach your children. These should be used according to their age. Gather in the living room and sit on the couch. Learn Bible facts and quiz children on them. Perhaps you could do it like an old fashioned spelling bee by having the children line up on the couch or along the wall. Start with the younger children and line them up in accordance with age. If the first child misses the answer, then the next one will be asked. If he or she answers it correctly he will pass the one who missed it. The object is to see who is at the head of the line when the quiz is over.

Read through the Bible letting each child take his turn reading. This works better for older children. If the children have questions about things in the passage read, take time to answer the questions or to search for the answers. Vary what you do so the children will not become bored with the same thing every time. Assign the children memory verses or perhaps even work on memorizing great chapters of the Bible such as the 23rd Psalm or the Sermon on the Mount. As the children grow older, memorize some of the shorter books of the New Testament.

Teach your children to pray. Pray with them in your daily devotional/Bible class, but also teach them to pray at bedtime. Giving thanks before every meal should always be done. A slogan from the 1950's says: "The family that prays together stays together."

Take time to play with your children. Do not think of your children as a nuisance. Read to your children. Listen to them when they want to tell you something and take time to talk to them about things that interest them. This is especially important when they enter the teenage years. Compliment your children when they do well and express your love for them (Mothers, remember not to hug your teenage children in public).

Corrective discipline is showing love for your children. Discipline the child according to his or her age and level of understanding. When a child is young, a simple "no" may be sufficient, but a little smack on the hand or on the bottom is a very effective way to let your children know you are serious. Don't let a child get out of control by waiting too late to begin discipline. Waiting until your child is a teenager may be too late to be effective (Proverbs 3:11,12; 10:13; 13:24).

Punishment may take different forms as children get older. Some effective means of discipline are taking away their phone for a week or even a month depending on the offense, grounding the child, taking away the use of the car for teenagers, etc.

An important part of raising your children is to teach them how to manage the things God has given them. They need to know the value of money and how to handle it. Teach them how to save. Teach them the importance of giving a portion of what they have to the church. Help them learn how to budget their money. You may give them a small allowance each week, but it is often better to let them earn it by giving so much for specific jobs. When they are old enough, it is good to encourage them to earn their spending money by baby-sitting, mowing lawns, etc. When a bit older, they may want to take a part-time job as long as it does not interfere with church and with school work. Before they leave home, they need to understand about checking accounts, saving for things they want or need, investments, and the serious dangers of overspending and going into debt. They also need to be taught the dangers of greed and selfishness.

Vardeman Forrester was a professor of psychology and sociology, a Christian counselor, and a preacher of the Gospel. He was also a husband and the father of several children. In a college course he taught called "Sociology and the Home", he emphasized the importance of families being together and doing things as a family whether it be going to a concert, movie or a sports event, a picnic or a vacation. He suggested families should develop "family traditions" which they keep every year. Birthdays, for example, should be special occasions when the one whose birthday it is can choose the particular meal he or she wants mother to cook, or if they go out to eat, the birthday honoree gets to choose the restaurant. Special traditions for the holidays might include having certain foods or trimming the tree. Such traditions create fond memories which bring happy thoughts and bind families together.

A well known Bible commentator, known for his wisdom and practical application of Scripture, offers the following insightful and practical advice:

"We must always depend on God and His providence: 1. For raising a family. If God be not acknowledged, we have no reason to expect His blessing; and the best laid plans fail, unless He crowns them with success. 2. For the safety of a family or a city. 'Except the Lord keep the city, the watchmen, though they neither slumber nor sleep, wake but in vain;' mischief may break out, which even early discoveries may not be able to prevent. 3. For enriching a family. Some are so eager upon the world that they are continually full of care which makes their comforts bitter and their lives a burden. All this to get money; but all in vain, except God prospers them; while those who love the Lord, using due diligence in their lawful callings, and casting all their care upon Him, have needful success without uneasiness or vexation. Our care must be to keep ourselves in the love of God; then we may be easy, whether we have little or much of this world. But we must use the proper means very diligently. Children are God's gifts, 'a heritage and a reward' and are to be accounted blessings, and not burdens; He who sends mouths will send meat, if we trust in Him…. Yet, if trained according to God's Word, they generally prove the best defense in declining years, remembering their obligations to their parents, and taking care of them in old age" **(Psalm 127, Matthew Henry's Concise Bible Commentary (christianity.com).**

REVIEW QUESTIONS

1. What is the primary responsibility of parents in this life?

2. When should parents begin training a child?

3. What is the meaning of "Do not provoke your children to wrath"?

4. What should be parents' number one priority?

5. What kind of spiritual training did Timothy have growing up? When did his spiritual training begin?

6. What are some of the ways you can teach your family in a devotional/Bible study?

7. What should always be done before every meal?

8. What should parents take time to do with their children?

9. A child should be disciplined according to his_____ and his

   _____.

10. Children should be taught how to _____ their money.

11. What are some effective means of disciplining older children?

12. Vardeman Forrester suggested families should develop _____

    _____ .

13. What are some household chores that children need to be taught how to do?

14. We should never think of our children as a _____.

15. _____ _____ is showing love for your children.

16. Matthew Henry said, "He who sends _____ will send

    _____ if we trust Him."

Chapter 11:   SATAN'S ATTACKS ON THE HOME (1)

Christians face a great, evil enemy who is filled with hate and seeks our downfall. This enemy's eternal destiny has already been determined by Almighty God. At the Last Day, he will be cast into the "lake which burns with fire and brimstone" along with all who have been led astray by him (Revelation 20:10,15; 21:8). This enemy is known by many names in the Bible. These names are descriptive of his vile and vicious nature. He is most commonly known as Satan, which means adversary or opponent (Job 1:6; Matthew 4:10), and the Devil, which means accuser (Matthew 4:1; 1 Peter 5:8,9). Among other descriptive titles he is called "the tempter" (Matthew 4:3), "the wicked one" (Matthew 13:19), "a murderer" and "the father of lies" (John 8:44), "the ruler of this world" (John 12:31), "the god of this age" (2 Corinthians 4:4), "the serpent (Genesis 3:1-8; Revelation 12:9), and "a great dragon" (Revelation 12:9,17).

Satan uses many tactics and tricks to enslave men by tempting them to sin and thereby become his servants (Ephesians 6:11,12). We must "resist the Devil and he will flee from us" (James 4:7). Since the home is the oldest and most basic of the three institutions ordained by God for man's happiness in this world, and it is also the basic building block of both the civil state and the church of Christ, Satan is determined to destroy it in any way he can.

In this chapter and the one following, we shall look at ten of the major efforts currently being utilized by the Devil to destroy the home as God ordained it at the beginning of the world. These ten efforts of Satan will be discussed in alphabetical order, not necessarily in order of the threat they pose to the home.

Abortion and euthanasia are a gross disrespect for human life as God created it. Webster's New World Dictionary defines abortion as "expulsion of a fetus from the womb before it is sufficiently developed to survive; miscarriage: called criminal abortion when unlawfully induced." Until the 1973 decision of the Supreme Court of the United States in the case of Roe Versus Wade, abortion, unless medically induced to save the life of the mother, was a serious crime in nearly all nations where Christianity had a strong presence. It was generally and correctly understood that "the fetus" was a living human being in the beginning stages of development.

The Bible, in both the Old and New Testaments, clearly teaches that the child in the mother's womb is a human being from the moment of conception. The death penalty, which is the penalty for murder, was imposed on a man who caused a pregnant woman to abort her child (Genesis 9:6; Exodus 21:22-25). In both Testaments the unborn baby in the mother's womb is described as a child. The Bible speaks of various mothers who are pregnant as "being with child" (Genesis 16:11; 19:36; 38:24,25; Exodus 21:22; 1 Samuel 4:19; Ecclesiastes 11:5; Isaiah 26:17,18; Jeremiah 4:31; Amos 1:13; Matthew 1:18).

John the immerser was "filled with the Holy Spirit, even from his mother's womb"

(Luke 1:15). When Mary, mother of Jesus, visited her kinswoman, Elizabeth, who was to become the mother of John, we are told that when Elizabeth heard the greeting of Mary, "the babe leaped in her womb for joy" (Luke 1:41-44). When Mary became pregnant with Jesus, she was said to be "with child" (Luke 2:5). If the fetus is not a child from the moment of conception, then these Scriptures are wrong! If the fetus is not a child from the time of conception, then at what point does he become a child?

Abortion is a clear violation of God's first command to mankind "to be fruitful and multiply; fill the earth and subdue it" (Genesis 1:28; 9:7). If the fetus in the mother's womb is indeed a child (and he is!), then the willful killing of that child is nothing less than premeditated murder! Ancient cultures such as that of the Roman Empire practiced the exposure of their unwanted babies to the elements of nature. Such infants were taken out into the forest, desert or mountains and abandoned to die of thirst and starvation, cold or heat, or the ravages of savage wild beasts. Civilized people are horrified at such practices today, but is the violent dismemberment of a growing baby in its mother's womb, done by a skilled doctor who has taken an oath to preserve human life, any different than exposing infants to the elements of nature?

God has not changed (Malachi 3:6). He still "hates hands that shed innocent blood" (Proverbs 6:16,17). Abortion is the murder of innocent children, "the fruit of the womb," who are "a heritage from the Lord" (Psalm127:3).

Euthanasia is also the willful taking of human life and is used by Satan to get rid of the old, helpless and handicapped members of a family. Those who are deemed to be too old to be useful to society, or those who because of birth or accident are handicapped and dependent upon the care of others, and are deemed to be a burden to society, are simply put to death. There is a growing movement to euthanize (put to death by medical means or by depriving of food, water and air) the elderly in Western society. There is no gratitude for a lifetime of productive service the elderly may have rendered.

The Bible clearly teaches that all human life is sacred because it is given by God. Therefore, only God has a right to legislate who is worthy of life or death. Men who willfully and unjustly take the lives of others, whether the unborn, the elderly, or those handicapped and dependent upon society, are guilty of shedding innocent blood and will answer to God for this at the Judgment on the Last Day (2 Corinthians 5:10).

A second attack that Satan makes on the home is a growing **addiction to cell phones, social media, video games and the internet.** These things are not wrong within themselves. They are wonderful tools for communication and information as well as entertainment. However, it is the misuse of them that is a problem.

Let us note some actual cases of individuals who were addicted to their smart phones, social media or video games. First, a wife and mother neglected her husband and children because she spent many hours daily in communication with "friends" on social media while her own family suffered for lack of her attention. Second, a married man with teenage children "trolled the internet" looking for women. He eventually left his family for a divorcee he met on the internet. Third, a grandfather complained that family holiday gatherings, which included four generations, were no longer the happy occasions they once were because no one talked to anybody else. They all sat together in the same room but each one, young and old alike, was busy with his smart phone. They were little different from strangers sitting in an airport lounge waiting for a flight. Fourth, a couple had taken their son, who was home from college for the holidays, to a movie. They were all three observed lost in their smart phones while waiting for the movie to start. Fifth, a young father was left in charge of his two little daughters while their mother was at work. He paid little attention to the girls for he was busy playing video games. When they tried to get his attention, he spanked them. Sixth, a girl in her early teens was communicating with an older man on social media. He arranged to meet her before her mother learned what was planned and put a stop to it. Seventh, numerous examples could be given of people who have supposedly come to church to worship God but instead sit in the assembly checking email, texting, or playing games on their smart phones or other hand held technology. Eighth, Christians have been known to post indecent photos of themselves, use filthy or blasphemous language, gossip, fuss and feud, and criticize the Lord's church before the world on social media.

What can parents do about their children abusing these electronic devices? First, they must set a proper example themselves before their children in the use of modern technology. Second, parents must teach their children to "guard their hearts with all diligence for out of it spring the issues of life" (Proverbs 4:23). Third, parents should not permit their children to take their phones and tablets to Bible study and church. The temptation may be too much for them to play with these electronic devices and they are, therefore, distracted from study or worship. Why not give your children a nice printed edition of the Bible and require them to leave their phones, etc. at home and take their Bible to worship?

At home, to prevent your children from going to websites that are pornographic, or to engage in risqué communication on the internet and social media, have one family computer that is located in a den or other common room of the house where all the family has access. It is not a good idea for children to have their own computers, phones or televisions in their rooms where they can use them unsupervised. During family meals and on special family occasions, have a rule that all cell phones must be muted. If calls are important, callers will leave messages. Family time and family unity are much more important than gossiping with friends on the phone. There are times when all of us, adults and children alike, need to disconnect from the rest of the world and concentrate on things that are the more important such as worshipping God and spending time with family.

A parent who is a homeschool mother offers the following advice on children and their use of cell phones, tablets and computers:

Parents should start at a young age to teach children about the dangers of the internet. They should have clear rules for using any electronic device. There should be an ongoing conversation as they grow, especially in the teen years.

When children have their own phone or tablet, parents should have access to it whenever they want. Parents should discuss with their children about the apps they are using. They need to be aware of what their children are doing. Many children hide their online activity from their parents. Communication is vital. Parents can use parental controls on children's phones. They can also check phone records online to see when and with whom children are talking and texting. Parents should also check a device's history.

All electronic devices should be put away at bedtime and not kept in the child's room. They can be placed on chargers where the parents can see them."

Addiction to alcohol, tobacco and non-prescribed drugs for recreational use is a third avenue of attack from Satan. Addiction ensnares many people and results in the break-up of countless homes as well as bringing great misery to many others. The dangers of using alcohol, tobacco and drugs should be taught to our children in Bible school, Christian camps, lectureships, at school, and most important of all, by parents in the home. If parents smoke, drink, or take drugs, they need to repent, confess their sin, and seek God's forgiveness. The strongest, most effective, and longest lasting lessons that parents can teach their children is by the example they set.

A fourth and very effective tool that Satan uses today to break up homes and leave children without the presence of at least one parent in the home (usually the father) is **easy divorce for practically any reason**. Children are permanently scarred by parents who fight all the time, physically and/or verbally. They are hurt even more deeply by divorce.

It is easier today in most countries to get a divorce than it has ever been. Many people no longer take their wedding vows seriously. Traditional vows which include a pledge to "forsake all others and keep yourself only to your spouse" are commonly discarded in favor of vows made up by the individual couples. They may vow to stay together "only as long as we both shall love" or similar sentiments. Many enter marriage thinking, "Well, if it doesn't work out, I can always get a divorce." We must get back to the old fashioned way of thinking, based on the Bible, that marriage is for life. When a couple have children, they have a responsibility to stay together for the sake of their children, if for no other cause.

Another stratagem that Satan is using very effectively today is **radical feminism**. The present day feminist movement is not about women getting the vote or having equal access to job opportunities. These things have been settled by laws in most, if not all, nations in the western world. Modern, radical feminism is a rebellion against God and the specific roles He has ordained and designed men and women to fill.

Modern feminism is a major contributor to the "uni-sex society" where men are expected to be more like women and women are trying to be like men. God made men and women different, both physically and psychologically. Confusion results when we ignore this. Ignoring the way God has designed us has resulted in transgenderism, same sex relationships, sex change operations, cross-dressing, uni-sex restrooms and locker rooms, etc. Surely, the great increase in homosexuality and lesbianism in the modern world is largely because of the confusion caused by feminism. Remember the words of Jesus: "Have you not read that He who made them in the beginning made them male and female" (Matthew 19:4)?

God made men to be larger and stronger than women generally. Men also have stronger, deeper, and therefore, more authoritative voices than women. Men are designed by God to be the protectors of the home and the providers for the family. God has given them the responsibilities of leadership in the home as well as in the church as we have learned in previous chapters.

Women, on the other hand, are meant to be wives and mothers. They are made physically to bear children. Because of their more sensitive and tender nature, they are also better suited to nurture children especially in their younger years.

Many marriages today are in a mess! Children are confused, hurt and angry. This has come about because men and women have forsaken their God given roles and rebelled against the very purpose for which God made them. We will never enjoy the happiness, contentment and fulfillment we all desire, and God wants us to have, unless we get back to the purpose for which we were created!

A sixth tactic Satan uses to destroy our homes is "**Hollywood**." Hollywood, California, USA was the center for many years of the motion picture industry. The term "Hollywood" came to represent the entertainment industry in general with all its illusions of reality. The term is used to include music and television as well as movies.

In the past, movies painted unrealistic pictures of life where the good guys always won, the bad guys were always punished, true love won the day, and life was lived happily ever after. Fights in the old movies were very obviously faked for one good guy in a white hat would easily overpower three or four bad guys in black hats. Sex was implied rather than shown. Couples were never shown in bed together and even married couples were depicted as sleeping in twin beds. If God's name was mentioned it was in a reverential way. It was never used in cursing or even as a mere byword. Four letter words were noticeable by their absence.

Today, it is different! Fights are realistic to the point of being sickening. Sex is blatantly shown. Nudity is not uncommon. God's name is taken in vain repeatedly. Four letter words are thrown in for effect. Storylines are often dark. If the movie is a comedy, the humor is rude and crude. All this is done in the name of realism, but it is meant simply to titillate and appeal to man's base nature. The result is that life often imitates art, or in this case, drama. People have become more irreverent, immoral, rude and crude as a result of the influence of "Hollywood."

The same evolution from the simple and pure to the sensual and vulgar has also taken place in music. Country music has gone from ballads lamenting unrequited love to songs about drinking, divorce, and unfaithfulness. Music is generally noisy and lyrics are often overtly sexual and frequently contain blasphemous or filthy language. This is especially true of rap music with its opposition to authority and Christian values. It used to be said that "music calms the savage beast." Today it would be more accurate to say that much of the modern music "stirs up humans to a beast-like frenzy."

Pornography is readily available today on the internet as well as in magazines and movies. Parents must guard carefully what their children watch. They must set an example. Let us heed the inspired words of the apostle Paul:

"Finally, brethren, whatever things are true, whatever things are noble, whatever things are just, whatever things are pure, whatever things are lovely, whatever things are of good report, if there is any virtue, and if there is anything praiseworthy - meditate on these things" (Philippians 2:8).

Christian parents are stewards of all that God gives us including our children. Stewards must be found faithful (1 Corinthians 4:1,2). We will all give an account to the Lord on the Last Day for our stewardship (Matthew 25:14-30). This includes the raising of our children. What task is more important than this? God has given us no greater blessing nor greater responsibility than that of raising faithful children who will one day inhabit Heaven. Ask yourself the question: "Will my children be in Heaven?"

REVIEW QUESTIONS

1. What are some of the names by which man's great evil enemy is known?

2. What does "Satan" mean?

3. What does "Devil" mean?

4. What is the destiny God has determined for Satan and all who follow him?

5. What is the dictionary definition of abortion?

6. Where in the Old Testament is the death penalty required for causing an abortion?

7. How is pregnancy described in both the Old and New Testaments?

8. What is euthanasia?

9. We must understand that all human life is_____.

10. If parents smoke, drink, and "do drugs," what do they need to do in order to set a proper example before their children?

11. How do parents teach the strongest, most effective lessons to their children?

12. _____ is a rebellion against the specific roles God has designed for men and women.

13. What are two specific roles in the home that men have?

14. What characteristics of women perfectly suit them to be mothers and nurture children?

15. What has the term "Hollywood" come to represent today?

16. Contrast movies of the past with movies of the present day.

17. What are some of the evils found in modern music?

18. Who has the responsibility to regulate what children watch on TV and the kind of music they listen to?

19. Have your children commit Proverbs 4:23 to memory.

Chapter 12:   SATAN'S ATTACKS ON THE HOME (2)

Christians face a great and evil enemy who seeks to destroy our homes and enslave our souls. Ultimately, if he succeeds, it will result in our being cast into "the lake which burns with fire and brimstone" with the Devil and his angels (Matthew 25: 41; Revelation 20:10,14,15; 21:8). In our last lesson we discussed six avenues of Satan's attacks on the home. In this lesson we shall notice four additional attacks.

Homosexuality is a sin which has been in the world for thousands of years. Satan uses it to pervert God's marriage plan of one man and one woman committed to one another for life (Genesis 1:27; 2:18-25; Matthew 19:4-6). Many ancient as well as modern cultures accepted homosexuality as a way of life. The cities of Sodom and Gomorrah in the days of Abraham four thousand years ago were destroyed by God because of this unnatural and vile sin (Genesis 19:1-28; Jude 7). Homosexuality was also condemned strongly in the Law which God gave to Israel through Moses at Mount Sinai. Under this Law, the death sentence was required for those guilty of this sin which the Bible labels as an "abomination" (Leviticus 18:22; 20:13).

Homosexuality was widely practiced and accepted in the Roman Empire in the time of Christ and His apostles. To show the need of the Gentiles for the Gospel of Christ, Paul speaks of the depths of sin into which they had plunged. They began by denying the evidence for the existence of the Supreme Being and descended into "vile passions" of male homosexuality and female lesbianism (Read Romans 1:18-32). Some of the heathen had been homosexuals, but they were forgiven when they were "washed, justified and sanctified" (1 Corinthians 6:9-11).

Our children must be taught the Scriptural truth that God created only two genders: male and female (Genesis 1:27; Matthew 19:4-6). We must raise our boys to be men and our girls to be women. We must not fall prey to the constant bombardment of movies, television, newspapers, magazines and books that there are more than two genders and that gender is not fixed at birth, but one is free to choose whether he (or she) is male or female.

A "homosexual marriage" is contradiction in terms. Marriage requires a male and a female, for only those of the two opposite genders can reproduce and assure the continuation of the human race (Genesis 1:27, 28). Paul's inspired teaching to the church at Corinth is as true today as when it was written:

"Do you not know that the unrighteous will not inherit the kingdom of God? Do not be deceived. Neither fornicators, nor idolaters, nor adulterers, **nor homosexuals, nor sodomites,** nor thieves, nor covetous, nor drunkards, nor revilers, nor extortioners, will inherit the kingdom of God" (1 Corinthians 6: 9,10).

Humanism is another tool Satan uses to deceive Christians and draw us away from God. Webster's <u>New World Dictionary</u> defines humanism as "any system of thought or action based on the nature, dignity, interests, and ideals of man; specifically, a modern, non theistic, rationalist movement that holds that man is capable of self-fulfillment, ethical conduct, etc. without recourse to supernaturalism."

Humanists believe man is the center of all things; the author of his own standard of conduct. He does not need or want God but desires to "do his own thing." More than 2500 years ago, the prophet Jeremiah rebuked such arrogance and ignorance when he wrote by inspiration:

"O Lord, I know the way of man is not in himself; It is not in man who walks to direct his own steps" (Jeremiah 10:23).

Humanism grows out of an evolutionary viewpoint that completely leaves God out of the picture. Humanism believes man is the most highly evolved of all life forms on earth. There is no place for a Divine Creator in the humanist philosophy. Man is, therefore, the master of his own fate. Humanists believe every person is capable of choosing or inventing his own unique standard of right and wrong.

Humanism permeates our modern system of public education from kindergarten to post graduate studies. There is no place for God, Christ, the Bible or the moral standard of Christ in the present day educational system. Teachers and professors are free to teach humanism and to ridicule Christianity and the Bible. Humanists especially seem to despise Christianity. They seldom know anything about Christianity and have a very minimal exposure to the actual teachings of God's Word.

Our children are being brainwashed by their teachers and professors who were themselves brainwashed as they came up through our public educational system. There is a greater need than ever before for strong, conservative, affordable, Bible centered Christian schools, colleges and universities where the Bible is taught, respected, obeyed and loved and is the very heart of the curriculum. When such schools are not available or affordable, parents have no alternative but to homeschool their children if they want them to be educated without having their faith destroyed.

Still another stratagem of the old deceiver, Satan (2 Corinthians 11:3, 13-15) is the growing practice of **couples living together and acting as husband and wife who have not been married in the sight of God and man!** Such couples are living in fornication (Colossians 3:5-7). They are guilty of committing at least one of the "works of the flesh." They will not inherit the kingdom of God (Galatians 5:19-21).

Marriage is both a civil and a religious contract. All men are obligated to obey the laws of God and of man. The laws of civil government are binding upon Christians unless they conflict with the laws of God. In that case, "We must obey God rather than men" (Acts 5:29; Romans 13:1-7; 1 Peter 2:13-17).

Christians understand that marriage is a covenant that a man and a woman make when they pledge their life and their love to one another. God Himself is a witness to such a covenant (Malachi 2:14-16). Those who violate God's laws of sexual purity by cohabiting without the commitment of a marriage covenant witnessed by God are guilty of the sin of fornication. Therefore, they stand condemned before God.

"Marriage is honorable among all, and the bed undefiled; but fornicators and adulterers God will judge (Hebrews 13:4).

We must teach our children that marriage is a sacred, life-long covenant between a man (male) and a woman (female) for life. We must emphasize to them, especially when they reach puberty, that they must "keep themselves pure" (1 Timothy 4:12; 5:22). They cannot engage in sexual relations before marriage without violating the law of God and bringing themselves under the judgment of God (1 Thessalonians 4: 3-8).

A final and perhaps the most common and most dangerous attack that Satan makes on the Christian home is **materialism.** By materialism we mean the desire to accumulate material things of this world above and beyond what we reasonably need to care for ourselves and our family, support the needy, give for the evangelizing of the world, and have a small and reasonable amount of savings for emergencies and the coming of old age when one is no longer able to work.

The Lord Jesus Christ understood the danger to our souls that a love of money and a continual craving for more and more and finer and better possessions pose to our faith. In fact, the Lord addressed the subject in His Sermon on the Mount. He began with a warning:

"Do not lay up for yourselves treasures on earth, where moth and rust destroy and where thieves break in and steal; but lay up for yourselves treasures in Heaven, where neither moth nor rust destroys and where thieves do not break in and steal. For where your treasure is, there your heart will be also" (Matthew 6:19-21).

Our purpose on earth is not to amass earthly riches and goods, but it is to serve God by teaching the Gospel to the lost and supporting others who take the Gospel to the lost (Matthew 28:19,20; Romans 10:11-15). It is also our purpose as God's children to care for those who are unable to care for themselves such as widows and orphans (James 1:27; Galatians 6:10). We must be "ready for every good work" (Titus 3:1). It is by doing these things that we will lay up treasures in Heaven. A wise man once said: "The only things we can take away from this life are the things we have given away."

The Bible warns often of the foolishness of making earthly plans without taking God and the brevity and uncertainty of life into consideration (Read James 4:13-17). Luke records an occasion when Jesus was teaching a multitude of people, but His teaching was interrupted by a man who demanded: "Teacher, tell my brother to divide the inheritance with me" (Luke 12:13). The Law of Moses which was then in effect gave very strict and plain instruction on the proper division of a legacy among the heirs (Deuteronomy 21:15-17). There was no reason for this man to complain unless he was not satisfied with his lawful inheritance and wanted more.

Jesus could see into the man's heart and therefore He knew his problem was was covetousness or greed (Exodus 20:17; Colossians 3:5). Jesus issued a stern warning to him:

"Take heed and beware of covetousness, for one's life does not consist in the abundance of the things he possesses" (Luke 12:15).

The Lord then drove this point home by teaching a parable which has come to be known as "The Parable of the Rich Fool" (Luke 12:16-21).

In this parable, Jesus told of a prosperous farmer whose land grew an abundant crop. When the farmer anticipated an abundant harvest, he began to think about where he would store all his grain, for his present barns and granaries were not sufficient to hold it all. The farmer came to a decision: "I will tear down my barns (storage facilities) and build larger ones." Upon further reflection, he came to another decision: "I will say to my soul: 'Soul, you have many goods laid up for many years; take your ease; eat, drink, and be merry.'"

Many of us would commend the farmer for his wise planning which made it possible for him to retire and "live on easy street." Millions of people nowadays work for years, invest, and save so that they can retire and enjoy a life of ease. Someone said that a century ago, the question most prominent in the minds of most people was: "Will I go to Heaven when I die?" Today, the most pressing and anxious thought is: "Will I have enough money to maintain my present lifestyle when I retire?"

The rich farmer was not said to be an immoral man or even an unkind one. Neither was he said to be a godless man. His mistake was one of stewardship. He forgot that all his blessings of abundance had come from God (James 1:17). He also forgot that he was a steward of all these things and must one day give an account to God for how he used them (1 Corinthians 4:1,2; Matthew 25:14-30). Additionally, he did not remember that he had a responsibility to use his riches to help others who were not so blessed as he (James 2:14-17; 5:1-6).

God called this rich man whom He had blessed so abundantly "a fool!" "But God said to him, 'Fool! This night your soul will be required of you; then whose will those things be which you have provided?'" Jesus then drew the conclusion: "So is he who lays up treasure for himself, and is not rich toward God."

The apostle Paul stated:

"Now godliness with contentment is great gain, for we brought nothing into this world and it is certain that we can carry nothing out, and having food and clothing, with these we shall be content" (1 Timothy 6:6-8).

A list of suggestions for Christians on how to manage our money whether we are blessed with much or with little contains some thoughtful and helpful guidelines on how we can learn to live on our income:

1. Make no debts except for necessary major expenditures such as a car or a house.
2. Make a budget and stick to it.
3. Give to the Lord's work as you have been prospered; a tithe is not mandatory in the New Testament, but ten percent is often a good beginning place.
4. Save a portion for "a rainy day" out of every paycheck; save for taxes, emergencies, and old age.
5. Pay all bills on time whether taxes, utilities, house and car payments, etc.
6. Pay credit cards in full at the end of each month; do not let your credit card debt escalate!
7. Live within your means; when tempted to buy something, ask yourself: "Do I really need it? Can I get by without it?"
8. Never buy anything you cannot afford! Count the cost!
9. Remember: You don't have to have the finest house, newest car, latest computer, most fashionable clothes, or take expensive vacations to be happy.
10. Don't store things you don't need and probably never will use; have a yard sale!
11. Raise a garden. Eat from it. Learn to can and freeze.
12. Eat your meals at home except when travel or work requires. Otherwise, take your lunch to work or to school. You'll be surprised how much you save.
13. Buy a late model, second hand car instead of a brand new one.
14. Shop at thrift stores for furniture, luggage, books, etc.
15. Cut your cable, internet and phone bills. You don't need 100 channels or all the "bells, whistles, and apps" that come with modern smart phones.
16. Have a reasonable amount of insurance but don't become "insurance poor."
17. Take family vacations close to home at parks; camp or stay in rustic cabins, hike, fish, swim, picnic, enjoy a campfire, have "fun" meals, etc.
18. Don't spoil your children by giving them the most expensive toys such as a new car when they are sixteen or graduate from high school. In later years, they will have the fondest memories of the good times you spent together, not the "stuff" you gave them.

Let us teach our children the best things in life are not purchased with money. Let us live by the words of Jesus and teach our children to do the same:

"Do not labor for the food which perishes, but for the food which endures to everlasting life, which the Son of Man will give you because the Father has set His seal on Him" (John 6:27).

REVIEW QUESTIONS

1. Why did God destroy Sodom and Gomorrah?

2. What was the penalty for the sin of homosexuality under the Law of Moses?

3. Is it possible that one can receive forgiveness for the sin of homosexuality? Give Scripture.

4. A homosexual marriage is a_____ in terms.

5. What does marriage as defined by God's Word require?

6. What is the dictionary definition of humanism?

7. Who is the center of all things according to humanism?

8. What is the standard of conduct followed by humanists?

9. Out of which theory does humanism grow?

10. How has humanism affected public education?

11. Living together as husband and wife without the commitment of marriage is the sin of _____ .

12. Marriage is both a _____ and a _____

   contract or covenant.

13. Who is a witness to every marriage covenant?

14. Define "materialism" as it is used in this lesson.

15. How do we lay up treasures in Heaven?

16. What question was in the heart of most people 100 years ago?

17. What question is in the heart of most people today?

18. What was the major mistake the "Rich Fool" made?

19. How do we lay up treasures in Heaven?

20. What will our children remember best and most about us?

Chapter 13:   GROWING OLD GRACEFULLY

"What should man do all his days under the sun?" This is the theme of the book of Ecclesiastes which was written by King Solomon, the wisest of Israel's kings. Some believe it was written by Solomon in his later years after he had seen the folly of his marrying foreign wives and allowing their false gods to be worshipped in Israel. The king experimented with many occupations, pleasures, and philosophies in his search for the purpose of life on earth. His final conclusion is not reached until chapter twelve. Therefore, one should be careful about accepting his tentative conclusions that he reached at different stages of his search. The final conclusion is stated in a simple and direct manner that no one can mistake:

> "Let us hear the conclusion of the whole matter: Fear God and keep His commandments, for this is man's all. For God will bring every work into judgment, including every secret thing, whether good or evil" (12:13,14).

Before Solomon stated his conclusion, however, he gave a warning and admonition to those who were young:

> "Remember now your Creator in the days of your youth, before the difficult days come, and the years draw near when you say, 'I have no pleasure in them'" (12:1).

From this point through verse seven, the king paints a picture in figurative language describing old age and the gradual dissolution of our aging human body which eventuates in the death of every individual born into this world. Let us notice each aspect of this process.

The "darkening of the sun, moon, and stars" is a poetic way of depicting the increase of afflictions, both physical and mental, which come upon us as we grow older. Often today we hear references to old age as "the golden years." Whoever coined that phrase must have been a younger person who had not lived long enough to experience the decline of his health and the weakening of his body as he aged. Those of us who have experienced this know that old age is anything but "golden", unless it has reference to all the "gold" (wealth) we spend on doctors, medicines, and hospitals to keep us alive and reasonably comfortable.

Solomon next spoke of "the clouds which do not return after the rain." This describes the gloom of winter which most elderly folks dread. It may also have reference to the "winter" of one's life when the infirmities of age envelop us and the prospect of death looms ever nearer.

The "keepers of the house which tremble" refers to one's arms which care for and protect his body. With the advance of age, one finds he has declining physical strength and stamina. This makes it harder to do many things which he once accomplished with little thought for it all came naturally and easily.

"The strong men bow down" refers to one's legs which throughout life have carried him quickly and easily wherever he wanted to go. Now that he is old, they no longer have the power to do this without greater effort or assistance.

"The grinders cease because they are few" refers to the loss of one's teeth, a common occurrence of old age. No longer is one able to eat meat and other foods which require strong chewing. With one's diet limited as a result, the enjoyment of eating is lessened or lost and one does not receive the nutrition needed to maintain good health.

"Those that look through the windows grow dim" has reference to the gradual loss of eyesight as one ages. Cataracts, glaucoma, and macular degeneration as well as other optical problems become more pronounced as one grows older. We are blessed today that we have eyeglasses and various surgeries to help with these problems, but in Solomon's day such were completely unknown. Until fairly recent times, it was not uncommon for those of advanced age to suffer from poor eyesight and even blindness.

"The doors are shut in the streets, and the sound of grinding is low" is describing one's mouth being closed as he masticates his food. Chewing is a chore because of few or no teeth.

"One rises up at the sound of a bird" vividly describes the difficulty many elderly people have sleeping at night. The aches and pains of age often prevent one from getting comfortable in bed. No more than the singing of a bird is enough to awaken one from a slight sleep. Perhaps this is the reason many older folks fall asleep during the day while sitting in a chair, watching television, or even during a conversation.

"All the daughters of music are brought low" is the result of one's losing his hearing. He can no longer enjoy the sound of music, or at least, hear well enough to appreciate fully its beauty. Such an individual may also lose his ability to sing as well as he once did.

"They are afraid of heights and terrors in the way." Because of weaker muscles and brittle bones which are easily broken, along with stiffness and soreness associated with such diseases of old age as rheumatism and arthritis, there is an increased risk of falling and doing serious damage to oneself. Lack of balance due to dizziness may also be a factor in the elderly avoiding heights. Climbing stairs have to be avoided as well as getting on ladders or stepping on a stool to reach upper shelves. Falls are a major cause of injuries in senior citizens. "Terrors in the way" simply refers to things in the way which are stumbling blocks to the elderly.

"When the almond tree blossoms" is a picturesque way to describe one well along in years. When the almond tree blossoms, it is snow white. When one ages, his hair loses its original color and become a snowy white.

"The grasshopper is a burden." The grasshopper is an insect that is light in weight and poses no problem for one in the prime of life, but to an elderly person even something as light as a grasshopper may cause discomfort for one who has constant aches and pains.

"Desire fails." The fleshly desires of the body which are so urgent in youth and continue into middle age lose their intensity as one becomes older. Sexual interest and ability wane with the passing years contrary to what sellers of aphrodisiacs claim in their advertisements. As one gets older, his sense of smell is not as good as in his youth. Therefore, his taste and enjoyment of food lessens.

When King David was able to return to Jerusalem after the rebellion of Absalom was put down, he wanted to repay Barzillai, an aged man who had supported him and brought him supplies when he needed them. David asked Barzillai to come to Jerusalem where he would entertain him in the royal palace. Barzillai declined David's generous invitation saying: "I am today eighty years old. Can I discern between the good and the bad? Can your servant taste what I eat or what I drink? Can I hear any longer the voice of singing men or singing women? Why then should your servant be a further burden to my lord, the king" (2 Samuel 19:35)?

After this vivid description of the decline of both physical and mental abilities in old age, Solomon states the inevitable conclusion to such a decline: "For man goes to his eternal home and the mourners go about the streets."

There was a time not so very long ago when many households were multi-generational. They consisted of the nuclear family of father, mother and their children but often also included an older generation of one or more of the parents of the father and mother. Sometimes an unmarried aunt or uncle would be present. Nursing homes, assisted living facilities and senior complexes are relatively recent institutions for the care of the elderly. In the past, family ties were usually stronger and family members closer than today. Children also felt more keenly their responsibility toward aged parents or grandparents than what is usually seen today.

God designed the home to take care of all man's needs from the cradle to the grave. Among our basic needs are companionship, sexual fulfillment, the bringing of children into the world and providing a safe, loving environment where they can be nurtured and cared for until they are grown and able to go out on their own. Homes also are designed to provide needed care for aged parents or other relatives who are no longer able to live on their own because of the infirmities of age.

The care for needy, aged parents is included in the commandment to "Honor your father and your mother" (Exodus 20:12; Ephesians 6:2,3; Matthew 15:1-9). The Pharisees of Jesus' day were hypocrites. They presented themselves as careful to keep the Word of God but actually created ways to get around commandments that they did not want to keep. They did not help their needy, aged parents because they claimed they had dedicated their possessions to God. Jesus told them they had made void or nullified the commandment of God by their traditions. Therefore their worship was in vain.

The early church took care of needy widows who had no other means of support. However, those who had children or grandchildren were to be cared for by them:

"Honor widows who are really widows. But if any widow has children or grandchildren, let them first learn to show piety at home and to repay their parents; for this is good and acceptable before God" (1 Timothy 5: 3,4).

Our parents brought us into the world, cared for, fed, clothed, educated and prepared us for life. They provided love and discipline and worked hard and sacrificed that we might have the things we needed. It is fitting and proper that we should look after them if they become helpless by reason of age or illness.

Children are a blessing from God (Psalm 127: 3-5). The same is also true of grandchildren. Psalm 128 pronounces a blessing upon those who fear the Lord and walk in His way. This blessing includes having children and concludes by saying:

"The Lord bless you out of Zion, and may you see the good of Jerusalem all the days of your life. Yes, may you see your children's children" (verse 6).

King Solomon wrote: "Children's children (grandchildren) are the crown of old men, and the glory of children is their father" (Proverbs 17:6). Someone observed: "Grandchildren are a gift that God gives to parents to reward them for having children."

Grandparents can have a wonderful influence for good on their grandchildren as well as receive great happiness from them. A helpful list of "do's and don't's" for grandparents in regard to their grandchildren will help us gain the maximum enjoyment from them and be the right kind of influence in their lives.

1.   Do be a good example before your grandchildren for they look up to you, admire you and will imitate you. Always model the best Christian behavior before them.

2.   Always take time to be with your grandchildren and make your time with them special. Spend time with them in conversation and get to know what they think.

3.   Be patient, loving and kind, but always insist on your grandchildren behaving themselves just as you taught your children to behave.

4.   Always make your grandchildren feel welcome and at home when they visit you, no matter what their age is.

5.   Teach your grandchildren about God just as Lois had a part in teaching her grandson, Timothy (2 Timothy 1:5; 3:14,15).

6.   If their parents do not take your grandchildren to Bible classes and worship, ask their permission to pick them up and take them with you. Read Bible stories to them.

7.   Pass on family history and traditions. Small children usually love for their grandparents to tell them things they did or things that happened to them when they were young. One little girl asked her father: "Tell us about the old days when you were young." Family history and traditions can be passed on to succeeding generations in this way.

8.   Don't try to replace their parents. Parents must have first place in their children's lives and grandparents should reinforce this. Remember that raising your grandchildren and disciplining them is primarily the responsibility of their parents.

9.   Don't criticize the parents of your grandchildren or do anything to turn the grandchildren against their parents. Praise their parents for what they are doing well.

10.   Don't argue, fuss or disagree with their parents in front of your grandchildren.

11.   It is nice to give occasional gifts to your grandchildren at special times like Christmas, birthdays and a rare special occasion, but don't spoil them with too many gifts, especially lavish or expensive ones.

12.   Remember the best gift you can give is yourself and your time.

13.   Be interested in what is going on in your grandchildren's lives. Listen to them. Allow them to confide in you and keep their confidences.

14.   From a grandmother and great-grandmother comes this advice: "Give your grandchildren lots of hugs."

Age has it problems, but it also has its blessings. Christians should not become grouchy, fussy, impatient, irritable or pessimistic in old age. We should use our retirement years while we are still able to be active by being involved in the Lord's work. Teach classes. Visit the sick and shut-ins. Prepare meals for those who are old, sick or lonely. Offer to run errands for them, mow their yard, or take them to the doctor.

One must remain connected with others. Go to your local senior center. It is a good place to meet other seniors and engage in a wide variety of social and recreational activities, most of which are free. Especially attend every service of the local church and be as actively involved in its work as your health and ability permits.

Take time to read the Bible every day. Take a course in a school of preaching in your area. Spend much time in prayer. Go on a mission trip to another country. Write to missionaries to encourage them. Remember that you are nearer your eternal home than you have ever been before in your life (Philippians 3:20,21). The goal is in sight! Don't mess up now! (1 Corinthians 9:24-27; Hebrews 12:1,2).

REVIEW QUESTIONS

1. What is the theme of Ecclesiastes?

2. Who wrote Ecclesiastes? At what period of his life?

3. What is man's purpose in life?

4. What is "golden" about old age?

5. What does "the clouds which do not return after the rain" represent?

6. What are "the keepers of the house"?

7. What are the "strong men"?

8. What are the "grinders"?

9. What is the meaning of "one rises up at the sound of a bird"?

10. What is one of the major causes of injuries in senior citizens?

11. What is the meaning of "desire fails"?

12. Why did Barzillai refuse David's gracious invitation to be entertained at the king's palace?

13. What does the commandment "Honor your father and your mother" include?

14. Why did Jesus call the Pharisees "hypocrites" in Matthew 15:1-9?

15. What does God give to parents as a reward for having children?

16. Name as many of the "do's and don't's" of grand-parenting as you can.

17. How can one remain connected with other people in old age?

18. What should one take time to do every day?

19. What are some activities that older members of the church can do to help others?

20. What should Christian senior citizens always remember?

Chapter 14:   HEAVEN: OUR ETERNAL HOME

At the end of a long hard day of labor in his fields, a farmer makes his weary way homeward. The anticipation of the warm welcome he will receive from his children and the prospect of a hot meal on the table prepared by his wife motivate him to quicken his pace.

With all assignments completed and the last exam taken, a college student eagerly heads home for the summer vacation. He looks forward to seeing his family, enjoying his mother's home cooking and spending time with friends he has known since childhood.

A soldier, deployed to a foreign field in time of war, counts the days until his tour of duty is over and he can return to the safety and security of his home country. He dreams often of that joyous occasion and the welcoming embraces of his loved ones when he arrives home.

In 1823, John Howard Payne, an American actor and playwright living in England, composed the lyrics to the classic song, "Home Sweet Home." The song became an immediate hit in both England and the United States and has remained popular since that time. Its opening lines often come to the minds of tired travelers who are far from home:

"Mid pleasures and palaces though we may roam,
Be it ever so humble, there's no place like home."

The three greatest sicknesses are said to be seasickness, lovesickness, and homesickness with homesickness being the worst of the three. An extended absence from our earthly homes fills us with a longing to return. Should not Christians also be filled with longing for their eternal home? The Lord was motivated to face the shame and suffering of the cross by the certain knowledge that a joyful return to His Heavenly home awaited Him (Hebrews 12:1,2; Psalm 24:7-10; Daniel 7:13,14).

The beauties and splendors of our home in Heaven are revealed in many descriptive phrases in the New Testament. Heaven is simply referred to as our **"our Father's house"** in John 14:1-3. Jesus had just eaten the final Passover with His apostles and had begun telling them of the things that would soon befall Him. The thought of their Master being so cruelly taken from them seemed more than His apostles could bear or even grasp. Therefore, the Lord spoke the words of comfort to them which are found in this beloved passage:

"Let not your heart be troubled. You believe in God. Believe also in Me.
In My Father's house are many mansions; if it were not so, I would have
told you. I go to prepare a place for you. And if I go and prepare a place
for you, I will come again and receive you to Myself, that where I am,
there you may be also" (John 14:1-3).

In his excellent commentary on the Gospel of John, Guy N. Woods points out that the Greek word which is translated as "mansions" in our older English versions of the Bible literally means "abiding places." The New American Standard Bible translates it as "dwelling places" and the English Standard Version renders it "rooms." We will not each live in individual mansions such as we envision on earth, but rather we will live in our Father's home which has rooms to accommodate all His children. Isn't it fitting that we who are God's children should live with our Father in His house? God's home will be our home in Heaven!

Our home in Heaven is also depicted in the New Testament as **a country in which Christians hold citizenship**. Generally, citizens have a deep affection for the land of their birth. They are proud of being citizens of their homeland and of the privileges that such citizenship brings. We must remember that Christians are also citizens of another kingdom, that is, a Heavenly kingdom. Paul reminds us of this in his letter to the church of Christ at Philippi:

> **"For our citizenship is in Heaven** from which we also eagerly wait for the Savior, the Lord Jesus Christ, who will transform our lowly body that it may be conformed to His glorious body, according to the working by which He is able even to subdue all things to Himself" (Philippians 3:20,21).

The New Testament also tells us that Heaven is **the place where our hope is fulfilled**. Paul emphasized this in his prayer for the church at Colossae:

> "We give thanks to the God and Father of our Lord Jesus Christ, praying always for you, since we heard of your faith in Christ Jesus and of your love for all the saints; because of **the hope which is laid up for you in Heaven,** of which you heard before in the word of the truth of the Gospel" (Colossians 1:3-5).

Hope is one of three Christian virtues which will endure to the end of the world (1 Corinthians 13:13). It will be fulfilled in sight in Heaven.

Paul wrote to Titus that he was "a bondservant and an apostle of Jesus Christ ... **in hope of eternal life which God, who cannot lie, promised before time began"** (Titus 1:1,2). Eternal life is a promise (1 John 2:25; Mark 10:29,30), but it is also set forth as a possession that a Christian can know he has (1 John 5:11-13). We presently have eternal life in promise and prospect. When the Lord comes again we will enter into the full enjoyment of it. Note Paul's explanation of the meaning of hope:

> "For we were saved in this hope, but hope that is seen is not hope; for why does one still hope for what he sees? But if we hope for what we do not see, we eagerly wait for it with perseverance" (Romans 8:24,25).

Two of the descriptions of our Heavenly home are found in Hebrews chapter eleven, a wonderful chapter which is rightly referred to as the "Hall of Fame of the Heroes of Faith." Some of the finest and greatest men and women who have ever lived have their names inscribed in this chapter by the Holy Spirit. One of these names stands out above the others in regard to faith. Abraham, "the friend of God" (James 2:23), received a double mention for two occasions when his faith manifested itself by his obedience to God.

Abraham is first mentioned in Hebrews 11 when he obeyed God's command to leave his home in Ur of the Chaldees to "go out to the place which he would receive as an inheritance and he went out, not knowing where he was going" (Hebrews 11:8). He did not expect to receive Canaan as a personal inheritance during his lifetime but dwelt in it as a stranger and pilgrim along with his son, Isaac, and grandson, Jacob (verse 9). The reason for his willingness to obey God is given in verse 10:

> "...**for he waited for the city which has foundations, whose builder and maker is God.**"

Later, Abraham's faith was tested when God commanded him to offer up his son, Isaac, as a sacrifice. He did not hesitate but at once began to prepare to carry out God's command. He knew God had said that the promise of his becoming the father of a great nation would be through Isaac. He believed God would keep His promise even if He had to raise Isaac from the dead (verses 17-19).

Why was Abraham willing to obey when given such difficult commands? The answer is that he was not seeking an earthly home but a Heavenly one.

> "For those who say such things declare plainly that they seek a homeland. And truly if they had called to mind that country from which they had come out, they would have had opportunity to return. But now they desire **a better, that is, a heavenly country.** Therefore, God is not ashamed to be called their God for **He has prepared a city for them**" (verses 11:14-16).

Some writers have suggested that the patriarchs and prophets of the Old Testament did not have an expectation of a reward in Heaven. Their hope was that God would reward their faith by giving them wealth and a long life on earth. These passages in Hebrews 11 plainly reveal that the Old Testament people of faith were motivated to serve God by their belief in Heaven and the hope of living there in eternity.

Another beautiful and encouraging description of Heaven is given by the apostle Peter. In the first chapter of his first epistle, Peter wrote:

> "Blessed be the God and Father of our Lord Jesus Christ, who, according to His abundant mercy, has begotten us again to a living hope through the resurrection of Jesus Christ from the dead, to **an inheritance incorruptible and undefiled and that does not fade away, reserved in**

Heaven for you" (1 Peter 1:3,4).

Peter first tells us we have an **inheritance**. When you were a child, did you ever pretend that a rich person died and left you a great fortune? Many of us have dreamed of the wonderful things we would do if we inherited a lot of money. Christians are "children of God and joints heirs with Christ" (Romans 8:17). Our inheritance is not on this earth "where moth and rust destroy and where thieves break in and steal" (Matthew 6:19). It is not affected by wars, recessions, depressions, fluctuations in the stock market, fires, floods, storms, etc. It is incorruptible and absolutely secure as long as we remain faithful to the Lord.

Our inheritance in Heaven has been **reserved** for us. If one is going on a long journey, he will make his plans for travel well in advance. This will include reserving passage on ships, planes and trains as well as hotels in the places he plans to visit. Barring unforeseen circumstances, he can travel in peace knowing that his travel and lodging arrangements are secure having been reserved well in advance. Our inheritance in Heaven is absolutely secure. No one, not even Satan, can take it away from us (Romans 8:31-39). We can lose it only if we foolishly turn away from God (1 Corinthians 10:12; Hebrews 2:1-4; 4:1; 2 Peter 2:20-22).

Heaven is also frequently referred to as a **kingdom** in the Scriptures. We must be careful to distinguish between the kingdom of God on earth which refers to the church of Christ (Matthew 16:16-19; 26:26-29; 1 Corinthians 11:18-26; 15:24-26; Colossians 1:13,18; Revelation 1:9) and Heaven, the eternal kingdom. Context will indicate whether the church or Heaven itself is being discussed in any given passage of Scripture.

In Second Peter, chapter one, the inspired apostle encourages Christians to add to their faith Christian virtues. He then admonishes:

"… be even more diligent to make your calling and election sure, for if you do these things you will never stumble, for so an entrance will be supplied abundantly into **the everlasting kingdom of our Lord and Savior Jesus Christ**" (2 Peter 1:10,11).

We enter the kingdom of God on earth when we are "born again of water and the Spirit" (John 3:5). One is born of the Spirit when the Spirit through the Word, which He revealed, begets faith in his heart for "faith comes by hearing, and hearing by the Word of God" (Romans 10:17; James 1:18; 1 Peter 1:22-25). One is then baptized in water into Christ and is therefore born of the water and the Spirit and is in the kingdom of God (Galatians 3:26,27; Mark 16:15,16; Acts 2:38, 41, 47; 1 Corinthians 12:13). The church of Christ, which is the kingdom of Christ on this earth, will be delivered back to the Lord on the Last Day when Jesus comes again, raises the dead, and judges the world (1 Corinthians 15:24-26; John 5:28,29; 2 Corinthians 5:10).

Our Heavenly home is called **the Paradise of God** in the Lord's letter to the church at Ephesus, one of the seven churches of Asia:

"He who has an ear to hear, let him hear what the Spirit says to the churches. To him who overcomes, I will give to eat from the tree of life which is in the midst of **the Paradise of God**" (Revelation 2:7).

"Paradise" comes from an ancient Persian word which means "a park or pleasure garden." It was used to describe beautiful gardens filled with flowers, fruit bearing trees, running streams, flowing fountains, and green grass. Kings in the ancient Middle Eastern kingdoms often had such gardens for their relaxation and enjoyment. The word "Paradise" came to be applied to any beautiful park or garden for pleasure. The Garden of Eden was called Paradise by early writers. "Paradise" is also used in the New Testament to refer to the place where the spirits of the righteous dead go at death to await the resurrection and Judgment. It is synonymous with "Abraham's bosom" in the account of the rich man and Lazarus in Luke 16:19-31. Jesus used it in this way when He said to the penitent thief on the cross: "Assuredly, I say to you, today you shall be with me in Paradise" (Luke 23:43).

In Second Corinthians, chapters 11 and 12, Paul is forced to defend himself when false teachers seek to discredit him and his teaching by denying he is an apostle. After speaking of his numerous sacrifices and suffering for the Cause of Christ in chapter 11, Paul adds the crowning proof that God had called him to be an apostle. He told of an experience fourteen years before when he was "caught up to the third heaven and heard inexpressible words which it was not lawful for a man to utter" (2 Corinthians 12:1-4). In verse 2, Paul referred to the place into which he was caught up as "the third heaven," but in verse 4 he refers to it as Paradise.

The Jews commonly spoke of three heavens. The first heaven was simply the sky where the birds fly. The second heaven was used to describe outer space where the sun, moon and stars are. The third heaven referred to Heaven itself, the location of God's throne. Therefore, Paradise was equated with Heaven itself.

Paradise in Revelation 2:7 has reference to Heaven itself. The righteous will go away into eternal life in Heaven following the Judgment (Matthew 25:34, 46). In Heaven, the Paradise of God, God's children will once again have access to the Tree of Life, which was lost when Adam and Eve sinned in the Garden of Eden.

We will notice one other figurative expression in the New Testament which is used to describe the wonderful place called Heaven. In Second Peter, chapter three, Peter tells of the coming Day of the Lord when the earth and the works in it will all be burned up. However, Peter assures Christians they have no need to fear:

"Nevertheless we, according to His promise, look for **new heavens and a new earth** in which righteousness dwells" (2 Peter 3:13).

Following the Judgment depicted in Revelation 20:11-15, chapter 21 opens with a vision.

> "Now I saw a **new heaven and a new earth,** for the first heaven and the first earth had passed away. Also there was no more sea. Then I, John, saw the holy city, New Jerusalem, coming down out of Heaven from God, prepared as a bride adorned for her husband. And I heard a voice from Heaven saying, 'Behold, the tabernacle of God is with men, and He will dwell with them, and they shall be His people. God Himself will be with them and be their God" (Revelation 21:1-3).

In his commentary on the epistles of Peter, John and Jude, the scholarly Guy N. Woods explains there are two Greeks words which are translated as "new." The first word simply indicates that which is young in contrast to that which is old. The second Greek word (kainos) is used here. It refers to that which is fresh in contrast to that which is old and worn out. The "new heavens and the new earth" are speaking of that which is fresh and new, not the old and worn out earth which was burned up and is no more.

Woods then summarizes by saying, "These facts seem to appear: (a) The present heavens and earth serve as a figure of the heavens and earth to follow. (b) The words "heavens and earth" are not intended to embrace all of God's material universe, but only that portion where His people dwell. (c) In the antitype, this limitation must be understood as a designation of where His people dwell, and not a detailed description of the future abode. (d) Heaven is the final abode of the people of God. (e) Therefore, the phrase **"new heavens and new earth"** must be understood as a designation for **Heaven** itself.

Our home in Heaven will be very different from anything we have known on earth. The occupants of Heaven will be the Father, the Son and the Holy Spirit along with the myriads of angels and the faithful people of God from all the ages. There we will see those men and women of faith mentioned in Hebrews such as Abel, Noah, Abraham, Sarah, Isaac, Jacob, Joseph, Moses, Rahab, David, Samuel, the prophets and many others from the Old Testament era. From the New Testament era, what a privilege it will be to meet and visit with the apostles and the disciples who knew Jesus in the flesh! From every century and from all the lands of the world there will be faithful men and women including multitudes of martyrs who have died rather than renounce their faith. What a privilege it will to get acquainted with them and learn of their lives and work! True Christians desire the fellowship of their brothers and sisters in Christ. We will have a never ending eternity to enjoy being with these wonderful saints!

There will be many things that we are used to on earth which will not be in Heaven. There will be no doctors, hospitals, funeral homes, or cemeteries because suffering, sorrow, pain and death will be no more (Revelation 21:4). There will be no armies in Heaven for we will be safe in the care of God Himself. There will be no need for policemen, judges, jails and prisons for the evil people will be in Hell (Revelation

21:8). There will be no sin because the tempter, Satan, will be cast into the lake of fire (Revelation 20:10).

We will never again suffer from natural disasters such as fires, floods, famines, droughts, hurricanes and tornados. None will be hungry or homeless. When we think of the glory and grandeur of Heaven, we cannot, with our finite minds and limited understanding, possibly envision all the beauty, joy, peace, contentment, and love which will prevail in that perfect place.

When Christians grow old and their bodies deteriorate, their strength fails, and they become discouraged and disenchanted with the ways of this wicked world, they long to go home to that place Jesus has prepared for His faithful ones. Don't you, dear reader, want to go to Heaven? Don't you want to enjoy now the peace and tranquility that comes from knowing you are saved and safe in the arms of Jesus?

Jesus died for our sins to make it possible for us to live with Him in Heaven. The peerless apostle Paul wrote:

"For you know the grace of our Lord Jesus Christ, that though He was rich,
yet for your sakes He became poor, that you through His poverty might
become rich" (2 Corinthians 8:9).

If you have not done so, you must be born again of water and the Spirit to enter His kingdom on earth, the church of Christ (John 3:5; Mark 16:15,16; Acts 2:38). You will then become a new creation in Christ (2 Corinthians 5:17). You will know the "peace of God which passes all understanding" (Philippians 4:7) and you can die in the sure hope of a home in Heaven.

When we contemplate the wonders of Heaven, we cannot but remember the One who suffered so much to make it possible for us to be there! **"Thanks be to God for His indescribable gift!"** (2 Corinthians 9:15).

REVIEW QUESTIONS

1. What is said to be the three greatest sicknesses? Which one is the worst?

2. Heaven is referred to as God's _____ _____ in John 14:1-3.

3. The word translated as "mansions" in some older versions of the Bible is better translated as _____ .

4. Christians are citizens of _____ .

5. Christians have eternal life now in _____ and in _____ .

6. _____ is twice mentioned as an example of faith in Hebrews 11.

7. T/F _____ The men and women of faith in the Old Testament did not have an expectation of a reward in Heaven.

8. Peter describes Heaven as an incorruptible _____ .

9. Peter also refers to Heaven as an everlasting _____ .

10. We must be born of _____ and the _____ to enter the kingdom of God.

11. _____ comes from an ancient Persian word which means a park or pleasure garden.

12. The earth and the works in it will be _____ up.

13. Heaven is referred to as a new _____ and a new _____ .

14. What are some things which will not be in Heaven?

15. Who made it possible for us to go to Heaven? How?

16. The phrase "new heavens and new earth" must be understood as a description for _____ .

17. What must I do to go to Heaven?

SOURCES

Bauer, Arndt and Gingrich: A Greek-English Lexicon of the New Testament and Other Early Christian Literature; Chicago; University of Chicago Press, 1964.

Berry, George Ricker: The Interlinear and Literal Translation of the Greek New Testament; Grand Rapids, MI; Zondervan Publishing House, 1973.

The New Analytical Bible (King James Version); Iowa Falls, Iowa; World Bible Publishers, 1973.

The New King James Version: Nashville, TN; Thomas Nelson Bibles; 1992. All quotations are from this version unless otherwise noted.

The New American Standard Bible (updated): Grand Rapids, MI; Zondervan Publishing House, 1999.

The English Standard Version: Wheaton, Illinois; Good News Publishers, 2002.

Matthew Henry's Concise Commentary: (christianity.com).

Jackson, Wayne: Before I Die: Paul's Letters to Timothy and Titus; Stockton, CA: Christian Courier Publications, 2007.

McGarvey, J.W.: Commentary on Matthew-Mark; Delight, Arkansas; Gospel Light Publishing Company, 1875 (reprint).

Rutherford, Vicky L: Advice on Electronic Devise Usage.

Strong's Exhaustive Concordance of the Bible: McLean, VA; Mc Donald Publishing Company, n.d.

Thayer, Henry: Greek-English Lexicon of the New Testament: Grand Rapids, MI: Zondervan Publishing House, 1966.

Vine, W.E. An Expository Dictionary of New Testament Words; Old Tappan, NJ; Fleming H. Revell Company, 1966.

Webster's New World Dictionary of the American Language (Second College Edition); Grualnick, David B. editor in chief: New York; Simon & Shuster, 1980.

Woods, Guy N. Commentary on the Gospel According to John; Nashville, TN; Gospel Advocate Company, 1981.

Woods, Guy N. A Commentary on the New Testament Epistles of Peter, John and Jude; Nashville, TN; Gospel Advocate Company, 1983.

Made in the USA
Columbia, SC
05 May 2025

57574152R00048